Entrepreneurial Wellbeing

Wellbeing is an integral part of living a fulfilled life. It is intimately related to people's capacity to work and maintain positive relationships. Wellbeing plays an important role in scholarly conversations and public policy debates. In this respect, entrepreneurship can be a source of personal fulfillment and satisfaction, which, in turn, can energise entrepreneurs to persist in improbable tasks that can become a force for a positive change in society. For example, new ventures are created by entrepreneurs not only to benefit themselves but to a greater extent to contribute to customers and other multiple key actors in society. Wellbeing is a complex topic that can be taught across a multitude of areas, including psychology, entrepreneurship and health. This book adds to the context of entrepreneurship by highlighting different types of wellbeing. In this book, the focus is placed on SME owners, and wellbeing and various ways of measuring it in different contexts are discussed. The SME owner is a critical stakeholder in economies, and therefore, the highlighted focus is on how they can apply and practically implement strategies linked to wellbeing which is deemed to be essential for business success. *Entrepreneurial Wellbeing: Perspectives in SMEs based on Gender and Immigrant Entrepreneurs* will provide views on wellbeing for entrepreneurs, students, employees and research audiences and will help them to further understand this multifaceted topic.

Jeremy Zwiegelaar is a senior lecturer in Enterprise and Business and a subject coordinator for the undergraduate Bachelor of Arts in Enterprise and Entrepreneurship at Oxford Brookes University.

Shelley Beck is a senior lecturer in Enterprise and Entrepreneurship and the subject coordinator for the MSc Business and Management programme at Oxford Brookes University.

Entrepreneurial Wellbeing

Perspectives in SMEs based on Gender and Immigrant Entrepreneurs

Edited by
Jeremy Zwiegelaar and Shelley Beck

LONDON AND NEW YORK

First published 2025
by Routledge
4 Park Square, Milton Park, Abingdon, Oxon OX14 4RN

and by Routledge
605 Third Avenue, New York, NY 10158

Routledge is an imprint of the Taylor & Francis Group, an informa business

British Library Cataloguing-in-Publication Data
A catalogue record for this book is available from the British Library

Library of Congress Cataloging-in-Publication Data
Names: Zwiegelaar, Jeremy, editor. | Beck, Shelley, editor.
Title: Entrepreneurial wellbeing : perspectives in SMEs based on gender and immigrant entrepreneurs / edited by Jeremy Zwiegelaar and Shelley Beck.
Description: Abingdon, Oxon ; New York, NY : Routledge, 2025. | Includes bibliographical references and index.
Identifiers: LCCN 2024030875 (print) | LCCN 2024030876 (ebook) | ISBN 9781032535067 (hardback) | ISBN 9781032535081 (paperback) | ISBN 9781003412403 (ebook)
Subjects: LCSH: Small business—Psychological aspects. | Entrepreneurship—Psychological aspects. | Immigrant business enterprises. | Women-owned business enterprises. | Well-being.
Classification: LCC HD2358 .E58 2025 (print) | LCC HD2358 (ebook) | DDC 338/.04—dc23/eng/20240712
LC record available at https://lccn.loc.gov/2024030875
LC ebook record available at https://lccn.loc.gov/2024030876

ISBN: 9781032535067 (hbk)
ISBN: 9781032535081 (pbk)
ISBN: 9781003412403 (ebk)

DOI: 10.4324/9781003412403

Typeset in Times New Roman
by codeMantra

Contents

Contributors by Chapter

Chapter 1

Dr Jeremy Zwiegelaar is a senior lecturer in Enterprise and Business and a subject coordinator for the undergraduate Bachelor of Arts in Enterprise and Entrepreneurship at Oxford Brookes University. He is the co-director of Oxford Brookes Research Innovation and Entrepreneurship Lab (ORIEL). His research areas are on nascent entrepreneurship with a focus on new venture performance. More recently he has considered the wellbeing of Canadian entrepreneurs using self-determination theory and current projects are being developed on the well-being of entrepreneurial teams in the Oxfordshire area. He is also a member of the peer review college for the EPSRC. He is currently a co-investigator for the DIGIT project over five years, which is investigating how Large Established Organisations are transforming to become more digitally enabled. His work has appeared in *Journal of Small Business Management*, *International Journal of Contemporary Hospitality Management*, *R and D Management* and *Strategic Change*, amongst others. Dr Zwiegelaar held academic positions in New Zealand and in UK universities over the last 12 years. Dr Zwiegelaar has a PhD in Management Entrepreneurship (Massey University, NZ).

Dr Shelley Beck is a senior lecturer in Enterprise and Entrepreneurship and the subject coordinator for the MSc Business and Management programme at Oxford Brookes University. Shelley obtained her DCom (Business Management) from Nelson Mandela University in South Africa in 2018 with her work that focused on the influence of parents on next-generation family members entering the family business. Her area of research focus is in entrepreneurship, particularly, family entrepreneurship and SMEs. She has been in tertiary education for more than ten years and taught various modules in the areas of entrepreneurship, marketing and research. In that time, her work has been presented at several international business conferences and journals.

Chapter 2

Dr Luna Dou is a lecturer and chair of the Assessment, Learning and Teaching Committee at the University of Buckingham's Business School. She is also a fellow of the HEA. She originally graduated with a bachelor's degree in engineering. Luna worked as an HR manager in the hospitality industry and subsequently received a master's degree in International Hotel and Tourism Management from Oxford Brookes University. Her research interests focus on social entrepreneurship, entrepreneurial wellbeing, trust and pedagogy. She was awarded a full PhD scholarship for her research which explored community engagement in social entrepreneurship, focused on an Eastern African country, Kenya.

Dr Wei Kang is a senior lecturer in Accounting and Finance at Anglia Ruskin University and a senior fellow of the HEA (Higher Education Academy). She is also an executive member of the BAFA (British Accounting and Finance Association) Special Interest Group in Diversity, with research interests in EDI (Equality, Diversity and Inclusion) and, in particular, gender diversity and substantial experience in curriculum review and development related to EDI. She is dedicated to promoting diversity in the corporate world and informing policy. Furthermore, she boasts significant industry consulting experience and has contributed to the "Futures by Design," a European Interreg Project aimed at assisting SMEs in the North Sea region with digitisation and green transitions.

Dr Nathan Zhang is a senior lecturer in Hospitality Management at Oxford Brookes University. Nathan teaches and researches the governance and management of risks/crises in both an organisational and tourism destination context. He has worked with major hospitality organisations on developing risk management and crisis communications strategies and authored academic articles on these topics.

Chapter 3

Dr Albena Pergelova is an associate professor at the School of Business at MacEwan University (Canada), where she currently holds the Board of Governors research chair position. Her research is interdisciplinary, and current research interests include social and emancipatory aspects of entrepreneurship, digital technologies and consumer wellbeing. Albena's research has appeared in a wide range of international journals across disciplines, such as *Journal of Business Ethics*, *Entrepreneurship & Regional Development*, *Journal of Business Research*, *International Small Business Journal*, *Journal of Small Business Management*, *Journal of Advertising*, *Journal of Consumer Affairs*, *International Journal of Advertising* and *Journal of Marketing Management*, among others.

Her research has been recognised with many "Best Paper" awards from international conferences.

Chapter 4

Dr Hannelize Jacobs has carved a notable academic career spanning over 25 years, encompassing both local and international higher education. Her professional journey is a testament to her unwavering commitment to teaching, extensive research and pivotal management and leadership roles. In her capacity as a pedagogical and behavioural scientist, Hannelize obtained an interdisciplinary PhD, a deep dive into eliciting, sharing and shaping tacit knowing and being for Strategic Innovation. Her scholarly contributions include a many great co-authored textbooks, research papers presented at local and international conferences and articles in scientific journals. Her research primarily focuses on entrepreneurship, ground-breaking educational methodologies and the strategic orchestration of innovation.

Dr Lizanne Gerber is a versatile professional with a Doctorate in Sociology from North-West University, where her PhD thesis focused on "The role and characteristics of the professional intercultural trainer in the South African workplace." She has a 16-year career spanning education and business, excelling as a trainer and lecturer across various disciplines and educational levels, from students to senior managerial professionals. Lizanne's entrepreneurial journey reflects her commitment to personal growth and innovative solutions in education and business. Her multifaceted career underscores her dedication and passion for inspiring positive change to help others reach their full potential. Lizanne's extensive experience spans the public and private sectors, allowing her to connect with individuals at different managerial levels, providing valuable insights and tailored guidance.

Chapter 5

Dr Wei Kang is a senior lecturer in Accounting and Finance at Anglia Ruskin University and a senior fellow of the HEA (Higher Education Academy). She is also an executive member of the BAFA (British Accounting and Finance Association) Special Interest Group in Diversity, with research interests in EDI (Equality, Diversity and Inclusion) and, in particular, gender diversity and substantial experience in curriculum review and development related to EDI. She is dedicated to promoting diversity in the corporate world and informing policy. Furthermore, she boasts significant industry consulting experience and has contributed to the "Futures by Design," a European Interreg Project aimed at assisting SMEs in the North Sea region with digitisation and green transitions.

Tolulope Oluwafemi is an assistant professor of Entrepreneurship and Innovation in Bob Gaglardi School of Business and Economics at Thompson Rivers University, BC, Canada. She is also an associate fellow of the HEA (Higher Education Academy, UK). Tolulope completed her MSc in Leadership and Management from the University of Sheffield, South Yorkshire, UK, and obtained her PhD in Management Studies from Bangor University, North Wales, UK. Tolulope is one of the co-founders of the Innovation for Social Good (ISG) research cluster at Thompson Rivers University (TRU). The ISG research cluster brings together faculty and students from a range of disciplines to create new knowledge about innovation that improves lives, organisations and communities. Her current research includes topics such as creating, leading and growing entrepreneurial ventures; immigrant entrepreneurship; and social entrepreneurship.

Preface

The success of Small and Medium-sized Enterprises (SMEs) often comes from the most unexpected places. Beyond the spreadsheets and profit margins, the gentle but powerful force of the wellbeing of people in that SME is at the cornerstone of that success (D'Souza, 2023). Wellbeing has become a central issue for SMEs, which needs to be explored in different contexts to enable a greater understanding. SMEs are responsible for two-thirds of all jobs worldwide and are the driving force of the creation of new jobs in both developed and developing nations (International Labour Organisation, 2019). Working from home has become a cause for concern as the boundaries of work and life are being diminished, leading to stress and reduced levels of wellbeing for entrepreneurs globally. The issues of wellbeing have received attention, but the processes and context have received less attention. Therefore, this book brings into sharper focus the challenges and struggles of SMEs in an international context and deliberately focuses on gender and immigrant entrepreneurs' wellbeing.

References

D' Souza. (2023). *Prioritising employee wellness: A smart move for SME businesses.* https://www.linkedin.com/pulse/prioritising-employee-wellness-smart-move-sme-d-souza-shrm-scp-/

International Labor Organisation. (2019). *The power of Small: Unlocking the potential of SMEs.* https://www.ilo.org/infostories/en-GB/Stories/Employment/SMEs#intro

1 Introduction

SME Contextualisation and Important Considerations

Jeremy Zwiegelaar and Shelley Beck

SME Context

Small- and medium-sized enterprises (SMEs) are determined by the number of employees in the organisation and/or the revenue that is generated (Razak et al., 2018). According to the European Commission (2024), a small enterprise has between 10 and 49 employees and a sales turnover of \$2,591,600–\$12,958,000. While a medium-sized enterprise has between 50 and 249 employees and a sales turnover of between \$1,295,800 and \$55,719,400, SMEs are seen as the driving force for country economic growth, sustainability and industrial development (Adebisi & Bakare, 2019). According to the National Action Plans on Business and Human Rights (2024), there are approximately 400 million SMEs around the world, which create 85% of all new jobs. The collective power of SMEs means that they represent an important part of GDP and are therefore the backbone of world economies (World Bank Group, 2019). Furthermore, the creation of new SMEs has the ability to generate new products, services and technologies and open up new markets and segments that were not there before (Global Entrepreneurship Monitor, 2024).

A UK Government study from 2018 highlighted the crucial role that SMEs play in their employees' wellbeing (UK Government, 2023). The study obtained the opinions of 500 SME employees and found that even though SMEs acknowledge the importance of employee health and wellbeing, relatively few provided structural support for their employees (UK Government, 2023). According to Stephan et al. (2023), wellbeing describes an individual's overall functioning and experience and can. One of the key barriers in providing the wellbeing support was the limited knowledge around the cost of wellbeing schemes and acknowledged that there was a need to assess the wellbeing needs of employees in SMEs (UK Government, 2023).

According to Klein and Schmitt (2021), wellbeing can be understood as a continuum, where a person's wellbeing can range from positive affect and having job satisfaction to illbeing and showing signs of depression and burnout. SME owners have been found to experience higher levels of stress and lower levels of support compared to their salaried workers and managers (Leung et al., 2020).

DOI: 10.4324/9781003412403-1

This is due to the fact that SME owners have a high level of personal risk of failure and juggle a variety of jobs and roles within the business (Leung et al., 2020). The effect of stress on SMEs can be detrimental to their wellbeing as well as the SME owner's health, motivation and ultimately their work performance (Khairuddin et al., 2019).

In the following sections there are two distinct SME focal areas, namely gender and immigrants in the SME context. In terms of gender, the 2023/24 GEM report highlights the contrasting disparity of support offered to women compared to men. A major barrier to female SME's success is the lack of support, and access to resources compared to men (Global Entrepreneurship Monitor, 2024). Women have been found to face several challenges such as access to financial capital and harmful stereotypes which many of their male counterparts do not face (Babson Thought & Action, 2023).

According to the 2016 Global Entrepreneurship Monitor (GEM) report, migrants have much higher levels of business startup than the home population (Roper & Hart, 2016). The GEM report further highlights that the percentage of immigrants starting their own business is around three times higher than life long residents (Enterprise research centre, 2016). This highlights the key role that immigrants play in their host countries and the opportunities they provide for society. For this reason the focus is placed on immigrant SMEs in this book.

This book showcases research that focuses on gender and immigrant entrepreneurship in order to provide further insights and considerations for entrepreneurs, policy makers, universities and development corporations in providing further support and access. In the next section current research issues based on gender and immigrant entrepreneurs are presented.

SME Gender Context

Currently, the emphasis on women's entrepreneurship has garnered more interest from supporting partners, governments and key stakeholders. Entrepreneurial women are individuals who launch startups with the intention of seizing opportunities. They possess a clear vision and a strong business orientation, demonstrating great persistence. Most importantly, they are also willing to take higher risks, driven by a spirit of adventure and a passion for innovation. There is growing research that contends that many women become self-employed for the flexibility that it affords, to manage work-family responsibilities, while others create ventures to avoid the "glass ceiling" in employment (OECD, 2021). The "glass ceiling" is about understanding that there is a limit to potential promotions and leadership positions in organisations. The focus and need to investigate the state of entrepreneurial women is borne out by the evidence that this group can have a positive effect on the economy of countries. The economy can grow fast, and poverty can be reduced by treating men and women equally. The literature shows that research on this topic constitutes approximately 10% of studies on entrepreneurship (Brush & Cooper, 2012).

A woman's decision to start a business is related to her socio-cultural background (Ahl, 2006). The gap between men and women in entrepreneurial engagement is often represented by the social roles and stereotypes that are culturally assigned to men and women. According to the social role theory (Eagly, 1987), gender stereotypes can be attributed to people and thus position them as being socially acceptable. When a role is associated with men, women who are not suited to the role because they do not have the necessary skills do not take on these roles (Henry et al., 2017). The behavioural differences related to gender-specific considerations and expectations could explain the different predilections of men and women toward entrepreneurship.

While there is improvement in the state of support for women's entrepreneurship and there is an increasing acknowledgement that more needs to be done to provide access and support, the rates of engagement by women entrepreneurs are still lower than the rate for male entrepreneurs. There is a concern that there is unequal access to resources, such as human, financial and social capital (Brush et al., 2004), and these barriers hinder the ability to address women's entrepreneurial potential (Marlow & Patton, 2005). Equally as important, the prevailing social and cultural attitudes around gender roles can lead to women self-restricting their business and entrepreneurship activities to certain sectors or professions and reducing their growth ambitions.

Business failure is seen as a continual challenge for women entrepreneurs. Across OECD countries, women were about 20% more likely than men to report over the period of 2015–2019 that a "fear of failure" prevented them from starting a business. These fears of failure are acute and often impact not just the entrepreneur but their families and communities too. On average, across the 49 countries surveyed in GEM (2022), 3.5% of women versus 3.8% of men reported exited a business in the past 12 months. Business exits were higher than startup activity for women in middle-income and low-income groups with similar ratios in high-income countries. More women in middle- and low-income countries exited a business than started a business in 2022.

In addressing the needs and considerations of the barriers to women becoming entrepreneurs and engaging in these activities, there is also a need to address the issues. Some of the ways to address these issues have been through the promotion of positive role models, which is seen as a key way in which policy can help to counteract traditional gender roles and encourage more women to consider entrepreneurship as a career (OECD, 2021). The need to promote women entrepreneur role models is most pronounced in Science, Technology, Engineering and Mathematics (STEM) fields (OECD, 2021). The positive representation of women in various outlets, such as media, direct interactions and learning materials in training and education programmes can increase the entrepreneurial propensity of other women (OCED, 2021).

In the chapter by Pergelova, she addresses the focus on the wellbeing of women in STEM and the issues of their wellbeing. Against this background, the aim of the research was to examine the experiences of women entrepreneurs and changes in their wellbeing as they move through different business stages of their ventures. The author used an interpretivist research approach by conducting in-depth interviews with women entrepreneurs in stereotypically "male"-dominated industries. The findings of the study provided themes which related to (1) taking ownership of oneself and one's personal growth and wellbeing; (2) tensions between entrepreneurial demands and family wellbeing; (3) fending off externally imposed views and practices and (4) satisfaction from contributing to the wellbeing of others. The themes were also considered in relation to the venture stage, which adds to our understanding about when in the business stage these issues arose.

Focus of Current SME Immigrant Studies

Immigrant entrepreneurship in SMEs can generally be considered to be about the endeavour of engaging in entrepreneurial activities by immigrants (Dabic et al., 2020). Immigrant entrepreneurs provide a key contextual entrepreneurial group to study for many key reasons. First, academics and scholars researching this area have proffered that with reduced command of language skills, relevant experience, resources or social embeddedness can lead to barriers to businesses being started and developed by immigrants (Constant et al., 2009; Millar & Choi, 2008). On the contrary, the immigrant entrepreneurs are over-represented in and have a higher proportion of self-employment than local born entrepreneurs in the host communities (Desiderio & Salt, 2010; Levie, 2007). A reason offered for this phenomenon is that they are confronted with high levels of discrimination in the job market and are thus naturally "pushed" into "necessity entrepreneurship" (Dabic et al., 2020; Soydas & Aleti, 2015). Given the forced nature of the entry into entrepreneurship, there is a need to consider the immigrant entrepreneurs' wellbeing, in more context-specific ways than their native-born counterparts. Immigrants have also been considered in more positive connections to provide competitive advantage for host countries because they offer skills and knowledge and can provide synergistic affordances from their international networks and promote trade between their home and host countries (Ng & Metz, 2015).

Contributing Factors

Wang and Jing (2018) reviewed the literature and found that identified work-related, non-work-specific and society-/community-related factors influence job satisfaction for immigrant workers which include workplace environment, job characteristics, worker characteristics and competencies and psychological state, language skills, cultural traits and acculturation (Wang & Jing, 2018). Based on these, many internal and external factors impact but one factor above all, job satisfaction, of an immigrant's wellbeing suggests the complexity of the topic and need for more research. A 2014 study of migrant entrepreneurs in the Netherlands found traditional economic sectors are preferred among those in the first generation, but as competitiveness in these traditional market segmentations (with low-risk options) increases there is a shift towards new markets, or newmarket orientation, which is influenced by network support systems, personality and history, management and marketing skills and business attitude (Kourtit et al., 2015). These migrant-founded businesses provide employment and innovation, and they influence the lives of the host countries' citizens (Kerr & Kerr, 2020). Again, highlighting the factors that make individual immigrant entrepreneurs unique as they adapt to a new country. Impact of country generalising immigrants into one category of simply "immigrants" or "non-natives" is a trend in the research on immigrant entrepreneurship; however, multiple studies highlight the impact of an immigrant's home country and destination country to differentiate their wellbeing. There is a continuing theme of subjective wellbeing because of increased income and business success.

Personality and Motivation

A Finnish study on wellbeing which involved interviews with immigrant entrepreneurs identified three main types of immigrant entrepreneurs: growth-oriented, investors and status builders who are considering freedom and stability seekers (Lilius & Hewidy, 2019). Rametse et al. (2018) investigated immigrants in Australia for their role in "startup motivation", thus leading to entrepreneurial capabilities. They found that, in their sample, immigrant entrepreneurs who reported higher levels of "individual achievement" were more capable of *opportunity recognition, innovativeness and proactiveness* (Rametse et al., 2018).

Barriers to Immigrant Entrepreneurship

A 2021 study in the rural UK, Lincolnshire, found socio-cultural barriers adversely affected immigrant businesses; therefore, adaptation was required to develop relational embeddedness within their communities through involvement with its social, structural and institutional frameworks (Hack-Polay et al., 2020).There may be additional barriers for immigrant entrepreneurs; however, Xu et al. (2019) found that involving Chinese immigrants in Australia found that cross-cultural capabilities that include the capability of psychological adaptation (emotion management and positive mindset) and socio-cultural adaptation (cultural learning, language skills and bicultural flexibility) can be leveraged to develop competitive advantage in international markets; specifically, they noted that the capability of emotion management helped maintain the overall psychological wellbeing. Limited or reduced access to financial resources from the host country was another key barrier to success for immigrant entrepreneurs (Malki et al., 2022).

Frameworks and Theories Used

In the extant literature there is a growing need to investigate multi-dimensional approaches (Ram et al., 2017) and the combination of immigration and psychological theories to uncover the role of psychological factors such as experiences of structural barriers (e.g., discrimination and stigma) on immigrant entrepreneurship (Dabic et al., 2020; Ramos-Escobar et al., 2022). In their review of the immigrant entrepreneurship literature Dabic et al. (2020) found the limited use of psychological theories to debate immigrant entrepreneurship, in spite of the general consensus acknowledging the view that the psychology of immigrants is different (Mahalingam & Haritatos, 2006). There are two main theories that have gained ascendancy, and they are the disadvantage theory and the cultural theory (Volery, 2007). Firstly, the disadvantage theory proposes that immigrants initiate their own businesses as this is practically the only viable way that they can survive economically living in their new country; it is, therefore, a form of necessity (forced) entrepreneurship (Dana, 1997; Chrysotome, 2010). Secondly, the cultural theories focus on specific characteristics of immigrants, rooted in culture, that make them more inclined towards new venture creation (Dana et al., 2019; Light & Rosenstein, 1995). With this backdrop we have positioned this research to advance a theoretical model which develops a psychological model of wellbeing within the context of immigrant entrepreneurship.

Methods Used

In the context of immigrant entrepreneurship, there has been a focus on quantitative, qualitative and a mix of the two methods. Quantitative approaches have explored topics like performance differences between immigrant and native-born entrepreneurs (Bird & Wennberg, 2016; Dana et al., 2019; Hopp & Martin, 2017). Some examples include a focus on global organisations (Lin & Yang, 2017), international surveys such as GEM (Peroni et al., 2016), commercial datasets like Dow Jones (Zhang et al., 2016), the Kauffman firm survey (Cheng, 2015) or surveys by universities (Ndofor & Priem, 2011; Qin & Estrin, 2015), amongst other sources.

On the other hand qualitative methods employing interviews have been used to investigate the role of social capital for immigrant entrepreneurship (Bizri, 2017; Dana et al., 2019; Katila & Wahlbeck, 2012), ethnic identity in immigrant entrepreneurship (Barrett & Vershinina, 2017), the processes of firms (Storti, 2014) and the impact of embeddedness in getting resources for immigrant entrepreneurs (Wang & Altinay, 2012).

Lastly, a mixture of the methods employed for comparisons between first and second-generation immigrant entrepreneurs have been using a quantitative (Beckers & Blumberg, 2013) and qualitative methodology (Hamilton et al., 2008). Likewise, the internationalisation of immigrant entrepreneurs has been studied quantitatively (Sui et al., 2015) and qualitatively (Light et al., 2013).

References

Adebisi, S. A., & Bakare, N. A. (2019). Survival strategies and sustainability of small and medium enterprises in a volatile environment. *Management Dynamics in the Knowledge Economy*, *7*(4), 553–569.

Ahl, H. (2006). Why research on women entrepreneurs needs new directions. *Entrepreneurship, 30,* 595–621. https://doi.org/10.1111/j.1540-6520.2006.00138.x

Babson Thought & Action. (2023). New GEM report underscores opportunities for women entrepreneurs. https://entrepreneurship.babson.edu/gem-women-entrepreneurship-2023/#:~:text=Among%20the%20key%20statistical%20findings,%2Dincome%20countries%20(11%25)

Barrett, R., & Vershinina, N. (2017). Intersectionality of ethnic and entrepreneurial identities: A study of Post-War Polish entrepreneurs in an English city. *Journal of Small Business Management*, *55*(3), 430–443.

Beckers, P., & Blumberg, B. F. (2013). Immigrant entrepreneurship on the move: A longitudinal analysis of first- and second-generation immigrant entrepreneurship in the Netherlands. *Entrepreneurship & Regional Development*, *25*(7–8), 654–691.

Bird, M., & Wennberg, K. (2016). Why family matters: The impact of family resources on immigrant entrepreneurs' exit from entrepreneurship. *Journal of Business Venturing*, *31*(6), 687–704.

Bizri, R. M. (2017). Refugee-entrepreneurship: A social capital perspective. *Entrepreneurship & Regional Development*, *29*(9–10), 847–868.

Brush, C. G., Carter, N. M., Gatewood, E. J., Greene, P. G., & Hart, M. (2004). Gatekeepers of venture growth: A Diana Project report on the role and participation of women in the venture capital industry.

Brush, C. G., & Cooper, S. Y. (2012). Female entrepreneurship and economic development: An international perspective. *Entrepreneurship & Regional Development*, 24(1-2), 1–6.

Cheng, S. (2015). Potential lending discrimination? Insights from small business financing and new venture survival. *Journal of Small Business Management*, *53*(4), 905–923.

Chrysostome, E. (2010). The success factors of necessity immigrant entrepreneurs: In search of a model. *Thunderbird International Business Review*, *52*(2), 137–152.

Constant, A., Kahanec, M., & Zimmermann, K. (2009). Attitudes towards immigrants, other integration barriers, and their veracity. *International Journal of Manpower*, *30*(1/2), 5–14.

Dabić, M., Vlačić, B., Paul, J., Dana, L. P., Sahasranamam, S., & Glinka, B. (2020). Immigrant entrepreneurship: A review and research agenda. *Journal of Business Research*, 113, 25–38.

Dana, L. P. (1997). The origins of self-employment in ethno-cultural communities: Distinguishing between orthodox entrepreneurship and reactionary enterprise. *Canadian Journal of Administrative Sciences, 14*(1), 52–68.

Dana, L. P., Gurau, C., Light, I., & Muhammad, N. (2019). Family, community, and ethnic capital as entrepreneurial resources: Toward an integrated model. *Journal of Small Business Management.* https://doi.org/10.1111/jsbm.12507

Desiderio, M. V., & Salt, J. (2010). *Main Findings of the Conference on Entrepreneurship and Employment Creation of Immigrants in OECD Countries.* Paris: OECD.

Eagly, A. H. (1987). *Sex differences in social behavior. A social-role interpretation.* New York, Psychology Press.

Enterprise Research Centre. (2016). Migrants start more businesses and are more ambitious to grow. https://www.enterpriseresearch.ac.uk/migrants-start-businesses-ambitious-grow-2/

Global Entrepreneurship Monitor. (2024). GEM 2023/2024 GLOBAL REPORT - 25 YEARS AND GROWING. https://gemconsortium.org/report/global-entrepreneurship-monitor-gem-20232024-global-report-25-years-and-growing.

Hack-Polay, D., Ogbaburu, J. T., & Rahman, M. (2020). Immigrant entrepreneursin rural England–An examination of the socio-cultural barriers facing migrant small businesses in Lincolnshire. *Local Economy, 35*(7), 676–694. https://doi.org/10.1177/0269094220988852

Hamilton, R., Dana, L. P., & Benfell, C. (2008). Changing cultures: An international study of migrant entrepreneurs. *Journal of Enterprising Culture, 16*(1), 89–105.

Henry, C., Orser, B., Coleman, S., & Foss, L. (2017). Women's entrepreneurship policy: A 13 nation cross-country comparison. *International Journal of Gender and Entrepreneurship, 9*(3), 206–228.

Hopp, C., & Martin, J. (2017). Does entrepreneurship pay for women and immigrants? A 30-year assessment of the socio-economic impact of entrepreneurial activity in Germany. *Entrepreneurship & Regional Development, 29*(5–6), 517–543.

Katila, S., & Wahlbeck, Ö. (2012). The role of (transnational) social capital in the start-up processes of immigrant businesses: The case of Chinese and Turkish restaurant businesses in Finland. *International Small Business Journal, 30*(3), 294–309.

Kerr, S. P., & Kerr, W. (2020). Immigrant entrepreneurship in America: Evidence from the survey of business owners 2007 & 2012. *Research Policy, 49*(3), 103918.

Khairuddin, S. M. H. S., Saidun, Z., & Hashim, M. S. (2019). Measuring the effects of work motivation on stress and performance linkages in SME. *Asian Academy of Management Journal, 24*, 1–15.

Kourtit, K., Nijkamp, P., & Arribas-Bel, D. (2015). Migrant entrepreneurs as urban 'healthangels'-contrasts in growth strategies. *International Planning Studies, 20*(1–2), 71–86. https://doi.org/10.1080/13563475.2014.942496

Leung, Y. K., Mukerjee, J., & Thurik, R. (2020). The role of family support in work-family balance and subjective well-being of SME owners. *Journal of Small Business Management, 58*(1), 130–163.

Levie, J. (2007). Immigration, in-migration, ethnicity and entrepreneurship in the United Kingdom. *Small Business Economics, 28*(2–3), 143–169.

Light, I., Rezaei, S., & Dana, L. P. (2013). Ethnic minority entrepreneurs in the international carpet trade: An empirical study. *International Journal of Entrepreneurship and Small Business, 18*(2), 125–153.

Light, I., & Rosenstein, C. (1995). *Race, ethnicity, and entrepreneurship in urban America*. New York: Aldine De Gruyter.

Lilius, J., & Hewidy, H. (2019). Serving whom? Immigrant entrepreneurs in a new local Context. *Fennia, 197*(2), 215–231. https://doi.org/10.11143/fennia.82821

Lin, X., & Yang, X. (2017). From human capital externality to entrepreneurial aspiration: Revisiting the migration-trade linkage. *Journal of World Business, 52*(3), 360–371.

Mahalingam, R. E. (2006). *Cultural psychology of immigrants*. New Jersey: Lawrence Erlbaum Associates Publishers.

Mahalingam, R., & Haritatos, J. (2006). Culture, gender and immigration. *Cultural Psychology of Immigrants*, 259–278.

Malki, B., Uman, T., & Pittino, D. (2022). The entrepreneurial financing of the immigrant entrepreneurs: A literature review. *Small Business Economics*, 1–29.

Marlow, S., & Patton, D. (2005). All credit to men? Entrepreneurship, finance, and gender. Entrepreneurship theory and practice, 29(6), 717–735.

Millar, C. C. J. M., & Choi, C. J. (2008). Worker identity, the liability of foreignness, the exclusion of local managers and unionism: A conceptual analysis. *Journal of Organizational Change Management, 21*(4), 460–470.

Ndofor, H. A., & Priem, R. L. (2011). Immigrant entrepreneurs, the ethnic enclave strategy, and venture performance. *Journal of Management, 37*(3), 790–818.

Ng, E. S., & Metz, I. (2015). Multiculturalism as a strategy for national competitiveness: The case for Canada and Australia. *Journal of Business Ethics, 128,* 253–266.

OECD. (2021). *Entrepreneurship Policies through a Gender Lens*. OECD Studies on SMEs and Entrepreneurship. Paris: OECD Publishing. https://doi.org/10.1787/71c8f9c9-en

Peroni, C., Riillo, C. A. F., & Sarracino, F. (2016). Entrepreneurship and immigration: Evidence from GEM Luxembourg. *Small Business Economics, 46*(4), 639–656.

Qin, F., & Estrin, S. (2015). Does social influence span time and space? Evidence from Indian returnee entrepreneurs. *Strategic Entrepreneurship Journal, 9*(3), 226–242.

Ram, M., Jones, T., & Villares-Varela, M. (2017). Migrant entrepreneurship: Reflections on research and practice. *International Small Business Journal, 35*(1), 3–18.

Rametse, N., Moremong-Nganunu, T., Ding, M. J., & Arenius, P. (2018). Entrepreneurial motivations and capabilities of migrant entrepreneurs in Australia. *International Migration, 56*(4), 217–234. https://doi.org/10.1111/imig.12452

Ramos-Escobar, E. A., García-Pérez-de-Lema, D., Castillo-Vergara, M., & Valdez-Juárez, L. E. (2022). Immigrant entrepreneurs: A review of the literature and an agenda for future investigations. *International Journal of Intercultural Relations, 91,* 170–190.

Razak, D. A., Abdullah, M. A., & Ersoy, A. (2018). Small medium enterprises (SMEs) in Turkey and Malaysia a comparative discussion on issues and challenges. *International Journal of Business, Economics and Law, 10*(49), 2–591.

Roper, S, & Hart, M. (2016). Migrants start more businesses and are more ambitious to grow. https://www.enterpriseresearch.ac.uk/migrants-start-businesses-ambitious-grow-2/#:~:text=The%20percentage%20of%20immigrants%20involved,EU%20and%20non%2DEU%20immigrants.

Soydas, Y., & Aleti, T. (2015). Immigrant and second-generation Turkish entrepreneurs in Melbourne Australia: A qualitative investigation of entrepreneurial motivations. *International Journal of Entrepreneurial Behavior & Research, 21*(2), 154–174.

Stephan, U., Rauch, A., & Hatak, I. (2023). Happy entrepreneurs? Everywhere? A meta-analysis of entrepreneurship and wellbeing. *Entrepreneurship Theory and Practice*, *47*(2), 553–593.

Storti, L. (2014). Being an entrepreneur: emergence and structuring of two immigrant entrepreneur groups. Entrepreneurship & Regional Development, 26(7–8), 521–545.

Sui, S., Morgan, H. M., & Baum, M. (2015). Internationalization of immigrant-owned SMEs: The role of language. *Journal of World Business*, *50*(4), 804–814.

UK Government. (2023). Incentivising SME uptake of health and wellbeing support schemes. https://assets.publishing.service.gov.uk/media/640f0d67d3bf7f02ff3f5744/incentivising-SME-uptake-of-health-and-wellbeing-schemes-report.pdf

Volery, T. (2007). Ethnic entrepreneurship: A theoretical framework. In L. P. Dana (Ed.), *Handbook of research on ethnic minority entrepreneurship. A co-evolutionary view on resource management* (pp. 30–41). Cheltenham and Northampton, MA: Edward Elgar.

Wang, Z., & Jing, X. (2018). Job satisfaction among immigrant workers: a review of determinants. *Social Indicators Research*, *139*, 381–401. https://doi.org/10.1007/s11205-017-1708-z

Wang, C. L., & Altinay, L. (2012). Social embeddedness, entrepreneurial orientation and firm growth in ethnic minority small businesses in the UK. *International Small Business Journal*, *30*(1), 3–23.

World Bank Group. (2019). Small and Medium Enterprises (SMEs) Finance: Improving SMEs' access to finance and finding innovative solutions to unlock sources of capital. https://www.worldbank.org/en/topic/smefinance#:~:text=SMEs%20account%20for%20the%20majority,(GDP)%20in%20emerging%20economies.

Xu, K., Drennan, J., & Mathews, S. (2019). Immigrant entrepreneurs and their cross-cultural capabilities: A study of Chinese immigrant entrepreneurs in Australia. *Journal of International Entrepreneurship*, *17*, 520–557. https://doi.org/10.1007/s10843-019-00261-4

Zhang, J., Wong, P. K., & Ho, Y. P. (2016). Ethnic enclave and entrepreneurial financing: Asian venture capitalists in Silicon Valley. *Strategic Entrepreneurship Journal*, *10*(3), 318–335.

2 Wellbeing of Chinese Immigrant Entrepreneurs in the UK

A Gendered Perspective

Luna Dou, Wei Kang and Nathan Zhang

Introduction

Whilst scholarly interests in entrepreneurial wellbeing have been growing (Stephan et al., 2023), limited studies have investigated the wellbeing of immigrant entrepreneurs. Compared to their native counterparts, immigrant entrepreneurs are found to encounter more barriers living, and doing business, in a less familiar environment (Hack-Polay et al., 2020), yet still making significant economic and socio-cultural contributions to their host countries, i.e. countries receiving immigrants and offering them domicile (Dheer, 2018). In the UK, Chinese immigrants form a significant group among immigrant entrepreneurs, ranking just after those from Ireland, India, Germany, and the USA (CFE/DueDil, 2014). However, Chinese immigrant entrepreneurs are arguably experiencing more challenges to their wellbeing due to substantial differences in language, culture, and institution (Wang & Warn, 2018). Despite this, the number of Chinese applicants for the UK's Tier 1 entrepreneur visa rose steadily from 2008 to 2019, which accounted for approximately one-third of all Tier 1 applications (HomeOffice, 2020). Given such growth of Chinese immigrant entrepreneurs in the UK, understanding and safeguarding their wellbeing are ever more important.

Recent studies on UK-based Chinese immigrant entrepreneurs have delved into various aspects of their entrepreneurial journey, such as the motivations behind starting their own businesses (Chen et al., 2019), the challenges they face in daily operations (Wu, 2021), and their survival strategies amidst the COVID-19 pandemic (Chen et al., 2023). However, to our knowledge, there appears to be a lack of research focused on their wellbeing. Similar scholarly work on Chinese immigrant entrepreneurs in other countries, including Australia – where research has explored entrepreneurs' motivations and the benefits they accrue (Patrickson & Hallo, 2021), Spain – where determinants of entrepreneurs' propensity to take risks have been identified (Rodríguez-Gutiérrez et al., 2020), and the USA – where studies have examined the impact of pre-migration business exposure on post-migration

DOI: 10.4324/9781003412403-2

entrepreneurial ventures (Liu et al., 2023), has also neglected wellbeing – a critical dimension of their entrepreneurial experience. This chapter aims to fill this research gap by presenting findings from a qualitative study into the wellbeing of Chinese immigrant entrepreneurs in the UK. We seek to provide a nuanced account of how Chinese male and female immigrant entrepreneurs perceive and maintain their wellbeing. Our interest in gender difference is informed by the notable increase in female entrepreneurship in the UK following the COVID-19 pandemic (Saker-Clark, 2023), suggesting a timely and relevant inquiry into how wellbeing is understood and sustained among this dynamic group of entrepreneurs.

Literature Review

(Chinese) Immigrant Entrepreneurs in the UK

Grasping the concept of an immigrant entrepreneur necessitates a foundational comprehension of the term 'immigrant'. While countries differ in how they define immigrants based on their citizenship policies, the consensus is that an 'immigrant to country X' refers to an individual born in another country who subsequently moved to destination country X at some point in their lifetime (Dheer, 2018), with the move being permanent in nature rather than transitory (Wadhwa et al., 2007). As such, immigrant entrepreneurs can be seen as immigrants who identify and exploit opportunities to create new ventures in their destination countries.

The UK boasts a substantial community of immigrant-led businesses (Wu, 2021), with their entrepreneurial activities outperforming those of native-born UK individuals (Guerrero et al., 2021). These immigrant entrepreneurs originate from a diverse range of countries, including but not limited to China, India, Ireland, Germany, and the USA. Most of their businesses are based in London, where recent data reveal that the numbers of immigrant-founded businesses in the capital are nearly ten times more than those in Birmingham, the UK's second most favoured destination for such ventures (CFE/DueDil, 2024).

Immigrant entrepreneurs are not only vital economic actors but also agents of social change in the UK. As a pivotal contributor to the nation's economy (Roberts et al., 2020), they create employment opportunities, revitalise underprivileged areas and deliver essential services (Jones et al., 2018). They are also highly innovative, taking in charge of half of the UK's 100 fastest-growing companies (The Entrepreneurs Network, 2023). As an agent of social change, immigrant entrepreneurs actively shape public perceptions surrounding immigrants, by demonstrating the positive impact they make on fostering social inclusion and integration (CFE/DueDil, 2014). Recognising such invaluable contributions by immigrant entrepreneurs, policymakers, and the media has been urged to celebrate and support this vital cohort, given the need for inclusive and pro-entrepreneurship immigration policies to sustain the UK's entrepreneurial ecosystem and economic prosperity.

Nevertheless, in contrast to their native-born counterparts, immigrants in the UK encounter distinct challenges in their pursuit of entrepreneurial endeavours. Specifically, some immigrant entrepreneurs, particularly those with limited human capital (e.g. education, knowledge and skills such as language proficiency) and social capital (e.g. networks), face greater hurdles in navigating regulatory compliance (Chen et al., 2019) or securing vital resources such as funding (Zhang, 2015). Additionally, there are immigrant entrepreneurs who struggle to expand their business beyond serving their ethnic communities due to niche market limitations (Wu, 2021).

Within the diverse spectrum of the UK's immigrant entrepreneurial community, the Chinese segment stands out. Yet, this group predominantly operates in sectors of the economy considered less lucrative, with a heavy concentration in retail, transport, and food services sectors that have low entry barriers (Yasin & Hafeez, 2023). Research focusing on Chinese immigrant entrepreneurs in the UK is notably scarce, primarily covering aspects such as their motivations for starting businesses (Chen et al., 2019), the obstacles they face (Chaudhry & Crick, 2004; Wu, 2021; Zhang, 2015), and the concept of business embeddedness (Quan et al., 2019). This gap underscores the imperative for more studies to better understand and support this entrepreneurial group.

Gender and Immigrant Entrepreneurship

Gender has consistently been a significant theme in the generic entrepreneurship literature, with studies highlighting distinct differences in the ways males and females perceive and engage in entrepreneurship. One key difference is that females are generally less likely than males to embark on entrepreneurship (Minniti & Naudé, 2010), a trend that seems consistent across various geographical regions and cultural contexts (Minniti & Naude, 2007; Wilson et al., 2007). Three primary reasons might explain this disparity:

1. Women tend to report a lower level of perceived entrepreneurial self-efficacy than men, meaning they are less confident in their abilities to initiate and run a business successfully (Koellinger et al., 2013; Thébaud, 2010);
2. Women are generally more risk-averse than men, displaying a heightened fear of failure that deters them from entrepreneurial endeavours (Bönte & Piegeler, 2013; Wagner, 2007);
3. Women seem less efficient than men in overcoming certain obstacles such as limited access to financial (Heilbrunn, 2004; Muravyev et al., 2009) and social resources (Koellinger et al., 2013; Verheul & Thurik, 2001).

In the scholarly field of immigrant entrepreneurship, the dimension of gender has not been extensively explored (Sun & Fong, 2022). A systematic review by Sarihasan et al. (2023), covering the literature from 2000 to 2021 on immigrant entrepreneurship, found only 20 articles that considered the role of gender. These studies frequently highlighted the heightened vulnerabilities of female immigrant entrepreneurs and the challenges they face compared to those of their male counterparts. For instance, female immigrants often possess less human and social capital (Chreim et al., 2018), encounter discrimination in their search for entrepreneurial opportunities (Malerba & Ferreira, 2020), and face barriers related to family roles and childcare responsibilities, which disproportionately hinder their entrepreneurial engagement (Collins & Low, 2010). These factors contribute to the observed trend of female immigrants being less likely to initiate their own business ventures (Brieger & Gielnik, 2021).

Regarding gender differences among Chinese immigrant entrepreneurs, the research is scant (Chen et al., 2015; You & Zhou, 2021). Chen et al. (2015) examined the relationship between social networks, Internet use, and the gender gap in business performance among Chinese immigrant entrepreneurs in Canada, discovering that the firm size of Chinese female immigrants was smaller than that of male immigrants. Additionally, the study found that female and male immigrants utilised and leveraged resources from their interpersonal networks differently, with women less likely to seek resources from men and more inclined to use their kinship networks. You & Zhou (2021) explored how gender and transnational dynamics affect Chinese immigrant entrepreneurship in New York City, revealing that Chinese female immigrants struggled more than male immigrants in acquiring social and human capital. Despite these findings, there remains a significant gap in understanding how Chinese male and female immigrants perceive and approach entrepreneurship differently.

Wellbeing and Immigrant Entrepreneurs

Wellbeing has evolved from the traditional notion of 'being well' to a subject of global interest related to human development (Sánchez-García et al., 2018). It is highlighted as a key aspect of the United Nations' Sustainable Development Goal #3 and is frequently measured in the official statistics of numerous countries, including those within the OECD. While the bulk of wellbeing research is rooted in disciplines such as psychology, economics, and sociology (Contreras-Barraza et al., 2021), the field of entrepreneurship has witnessed an exponential increase in research on entrepreneur's wellbeing over the past decade (Stephan et al., 2023). The significance of wellbeing for entrepreneurs has been well-documented (Stephan, 2018), and it has even been recognised as a criterion for measuring entrepreneurship success (Wach et al., 2016).

Two perspectives (i.e. hedonic and eudaimonic wellbeing) seem to dominate the entrepreneurship literature that examines the construct of wellbeing (Sánchez-García et al., 2018). Hedonic wellbeing, also known as subjective wellbeing, refers to happiness derived from achieving pleasure and avoiding pain (Diener et al., 1999). It underscores the presence of positive affect and greater satisfaction with life, as well as the absence of negative affect. Eudaimonic wellbeing refers to the degree to which a person is fully functioning and entails experiences of self-actualisation, meaningfulness, and feeling alive, thriving, and authentic (Ryan & Deci, 2001).

However, past research tends to treat wellbeing as a unidimensional construct and many studies only assess a single wellbeing indicator to make generalised claims about wellbeing (Wiklund et al., 2019). With a view that the nature of entrepreneurial wellbeing is multi-dimensional, Stephan et al. (2023) proposed an organising framework of wellbeing components by building on the hedonic and eudaimonic perspectives. The framework argues that the wellbeing of entrepreneurs is composed of two higher-level components: (1) positive wellbeing and (2) negative wellbeing/mental illbeing. *Positive* wellbeing involves satisfaction with life and work (also known as cognitive wellbeing), positive affect, and eudaimonic wellbeing. *Negative* wellbeing/mental illbeing encompasses negative affect and mental health problems. A unique characteristic of this wellbeing conceptualisation is that *positive* and *negative* wellbeing components are relatively independent of each other and both positive wellbeing and negative wellbeing/mental illbeing can co-occur. Therefore, rather than perceiving wellbeing as unidimensional that ranges from positive to negative on a spectrum, both positive and negative wellbeing need to be considered jointly and simultaneously to better understand and assess entrepreneur wellbeing. We advocate the wellbeing view of Stephan et al. (2023) in this chapter.

Despite the increase of wellbeing research in entrepreneurship, studies focusing on the wellbeing of immigrant entrepreneurs are scarce (Dheer, 2018). It could be posited that immigrant entrepreneurs might experience less positive wellbeing and more negative wellbeing/mental illbeing than their non-immigrant counterparts as they often face greater challenges in accessing and mobilising essential resources (Hack-Polay et al., 2020). Contrary to this assumption, Zbierowski et al. (2019) found that immigrant entrepreneurs reported higher levels of wellbeing (measured as life satisfaction) than non-immigrant entrepreneurs. Indeed, engaging in entrepreneurial activities could facilitate immigrants' integration into the receiving nations, thereby improving their positive wellbeing (Alrawadieh et al., 2021; Poblete, 2018).

To our knowledge, the wellbeing of Chinese immigrant entrepreneurs has not been specifically explored. Research on entrepreneurs in Mainland China indicates a general lack of awareness about wellbeing (Xu & Jia, 2022), with many entrepreneurs living with poor mental health and showing reluctance to seek assistance (Xu et al., 2021). This issue could be particularly pronounced among Chinese immigrant entrepreneurs in the UK, especially female entrepreneurs, who may face more stress and challenges related to entrepreneurship than their counterparts in Mainland China (and to male entrepreneurs). Such stress and challenges could negatively impact not only their business ventures (Sevä et al., 2016) but also their own wellbeing and that of their family members. The COVID-19 pandemic had likely intensified these difficulties as Chinese immigrant entrepreneurs needed to navigate greater adversities at both the personal and business levels (Xu & Jia, 2022). However, it remains unclear how their wellbeing was influenced by entrepreneurial activities during the pandemic and what measures, if any, they have taken to maintain and improve their wellbeing.

Data

The findings of this chapter are grounded in a qualitative research study. In 2023, a total of 34 unstructured interviews were conducted, consisting of 14 male and 20 female participants, whose ages ranged from 31 to 69 years. The decision to use unstructured interviews was intentional, aiming to enable participants to delve deeply into their immigration and entrepreneurial journeys (Gudkova, 2018). This approach provided rich, detailed insights that enhanced the exploration of their entire entrepreneurial process and wellbeing. The interviews varied in length, lasting anywhere from 45 to 90 minutes. All participants were first-generation Chinese immigrant SME owners, residing across various regions of England. Within the group, 14 were engaged in the food business sector, including 8 restaurant owners, 3 bakery owners, 2 takeaway owners, and 1 supermarket owner. The education sector accounted for 9 participants, mainly providing after-school tutoring (4), assisting those seeking overseas studies (3), and collaborating with universities. Additionally, 5 participants operated in the real estate sector; 3 in fashion retail, and 3 in other services, including accounting (1), tech sales (1), and marketing (1). Notably, 31 participants primarily served the Chinese market. However, approximately half of the businesses in the food sector also attracted a considerable non-Chinese clientele.

Findings and Discussion

This section presents the key findings emerged from the study and contextualises them within the existing body of relevant literature. It starts by considering the concept of wellbeing as understood by UK-based Chinese immigrant entrepreneurs. Following this, the section offers insights into the effects of entrepreneurial activities – both generally and specifically during the COVID-19 pandemic – on their wellbeing. The section then transitions to the topic of 'self-care' as an overarching strategy for maintaining and improving wellbeing. Where relevant, gender differences within the key themes are highlighted and explored, providing a nuanced understanding of the diverse experiences and perspectives among the Chinese immigrant entrepreneurs.

Perception of Wellbeing

There was a shared consensus among participants that wellbeing is best interpreted as '状态好不好' (indicating one's state of being is good or bad). Every participant understood what a 'good state' means, both mentally and physically. The mental state, they believed, influences the physical. Most of male participants' accounts centred on personal feelings of joy and sorrow (hedonic wellbeing) (Ryan & Deci, 2001), while more females touched on deeper themes of self-worth (eudaimonic wellbeing). This aligns with the finding of Patrickson and Hallo (2021) that women place greater emphasis on realising values and personal growth within the entrepreneurial context. A majority of the entrepreneurs shared the view that Chinese immigrant entrepreneurs generally avoid discussing their wellbeing, a reluctance deeply embedded in the Chinese cultural emphasis on maintaining one's 'face'. One male entrepreneur commented that *'your wellbeing is not just a personal matter, it's a public reflection of your competence'*.

A subset of participants highlighted the pandemic's impact in raising awareness about wellbeing, but only about half of all participants believed it is necessary to discuss or address it. Others felt passive to address it as '*time would cure most adversities and patience is the remedy*'. Conversely, primarily women in their 30s or 40s actively pursued an improved state of wellbeing and considered discussions regarding this aspect to be essential. They explained that the pandemic, witnessing the death of loved ones and the pain of familial separations, shifted their priorities towards health and familial happiness. They consistently mentioned that if their wellbeing is compromised, it adversely affects their children. When probed about the impact on their partners, two distinct responses emerged.

One response came from female entrepreneurs, whose husbands were originally from Mainland China. They claimed that their husbands tend to maintain a distance. Very few husbands noticed their wives' negative wellbeing indicators such as negative affect and mental health problems (Stephan et al., 2023), and even if they did, they seldom lent an empathetic ear, rather they belittled their wives. In contrast, female entrepreneurs married to foreign spouses (i.e. non-Chinese) received significant support from their partners, who actively participated in household duties and childcare, showed interest in their wives' state of wellbeing, and encouraged open communication. This prompted a realisation that female entrepreneurs should pay more attention to their own wellbeing. This contrasting observation might be attributed to a deeply entrenched societal belief in China, where female entrepreneurs are often regarded as incompatible with the traditional roles of wife and mother. Such perception leads to a general lack of familial support for women who aspire to entrepreneurship (Song & Li, 2023).

Entrepreneurship and Wellbeing

Quite a few participants expressed contemplation over their current intense work situation. They questioned, '*would life be more relaxed and joyful if I were not the employer, thus bearing less responsibility and risk?*' Entrepreneurship presents numerous challenges, especially for first-generation Chinese immigrants. They must invest more time and effort than locals to ensure the efficiency of every business aspect (Wu, 2021). There was consensus that during the initial stage of entrepreneurship, individuals faced the most challenges, making this phase particularly susceptible to experience negative wellbeing (Stephan et al., 2023). Language barriers exacerbated these difficulties as many entrepreneurs struggled to comprehend the nuances of legal regulations due to linguistic limitations. Additionally, the lack of fluency in English often hindered the formation of friendships with experienced local businesspersons and the establishment of a local customer base. However, persistence over a period of one to two years have lead to an improvement in circumstances and improved wellbeing. Therefore, it was evident from our data that the positive and negative wellbeing components are closely linked to the different stages of the entrepreneurial journey (Stephan et al., 2023).

The myriad of situations encountered during the entrepreneurial process are intricately linked to wellbeing as this journey can oscillate between elevating one's spirits to great heights and causing profound emotional downturns (Stephan et al., 2020). However, some participants felt that their wellbeing was worse when employed in other companies. As one claimed, '*despite the increased hardships of doing things myself, my general wellbeing is much better*'. Some women mentioned that they could finally engage in activities they were interested in as the broader environment in the UK supports female entrepreneurship. This contrasts with the situation in China, where few friends and family members would support their entrepreneurial aspirations. This brings into focus their motives for entrepreneurship. The driving forces may vary: inability to secure a respectable job, such as a white-collar position, or a genuine allure for entrepreneurial endeavours. The former scenario involves participants who, due to a lack of better alternatives, embrace their entrepreneurial endeavours with a sense of gratitude. They were often older, in their 50s or 60s, and viewed the hard work that secured their income as a fair trade-off. Such entrepreneurs, even when faced with pressures, tend to endure silently (Xu et al., 2021). Other participants made a rational decision to pursue entrepreneurship over traditional employment, recognising more lucrative and fulfiling opportunities. This includes those who successfully imported Chinese goods to the UK or catered to the increasing Chinese student population with educational services. They took pride in their achievements, which drove them to continuously innovate and challenge themselves. Preferring customer interaction over subordinate roles, their pursuit of personal success often led to overexertion, necessitating family understanding and support for their wellbeing.

Within the demographic of proactive entrepreneurs who made rational decisions, the experiences of men and women were markedly distinct. Male entrepreneurs often thanked their partners, usually dedicated Chinese wives, for managing household and childcare duties, which allowed them to focus on the business. In contrast, female entrepreneurs reported a lack of such support from their Chinese partners. Many encountered relationship breakdowns due to their partner's lack of understanding, leading to single motherhood and independent business management. Some only found support after remarrying non-Chinese partners, who often had aspirations to, or understanding of, entrepreneurship themselves, thus being more willing to provide emotional and resource support. In China, achieving career success tends to diminish women's competitiveness in marriage (Song & Li, 2023), but our data show that in the UK such women are more likely to find a happy marriage.

Despite their capabilities and aspirations for self-fulfilment, Chinese female immigrant entrepreneurs face significant challenges, highlighting the importance of a supportive family environment (Sarihasan et al., 2023). Some participants entered the education sector, hoping their children could benefit from the acquired knowledge and resources. Yet they faced increased challenges due to working in unfamiliar fields, which often led to instability in their wellbeing. In contrast, male entrepreneurs usually focused on financial gains or personal achievement. They perceived that female entrepreneurs face no greater challenges than men, attributing this to gender equality and men's familial contributions. This reveals a lack of awareness of the extensive time and effort women invest in family and childcare responsibilities. Societal expectations in China place a woman's primary focus on her home and children's education, often viewing the pursuit of personal career goals as selfish (Song & Li, 2023). These women, valuing their children's education highly, experienced added stress and a heightened awareness of their wellbeing.

Effect of the COVID-19 Pandemic on Wellbeing

In line with previous research (Xu & Jia, 2022), our data suggest that the pandemic intensified the pressures on entrepreneurship due to the disruption in normal operations and the uncertainty of governmental policies. The ambiguity regarding the future left many entrepreneurs in a dilemma: '*should I abandon my current venture and pursue alternative professions, or should I persevere?*' '*If I was to change professions, which industries offer promising prospects?*' '*If I choose to persist, for how long should I do so?*' Numerous questions loomed in the minds of the participants, with such uncertainties leading to heightened anxiety and distress, subsequently affecting their wellbeing. Some restaurants temporarily transitioned to take-away services, but some of their dishes were not necessarily suited for delivery, resulting in limited revenues. '*Fortunately, there were government subsidies, otherwise, many Chinese restaurants would have gone bankrupt*', remarked one entrepreneur. Meanwhile, businesses that relied on face-to-face interactions, such as hairdressing and beauty services, had seen their operations fail almost.

Conversely, certain sectors, like home renovation and online education, had seen a surge in demand during the pandemic. Some participants in these booming sectors even became workaholics, which was not beneficial for their wellbeing (Stephan et al., 2023). There was a common sentiment: despite substantial profits, the overwhelming workload had overshadowed quality time with their families. One male entrepreneur shared,

> *during the pandemic, I was constantly travelling for renovation projects with my team, returning home merely to sleep. I had little energy for anything else. My children were attending online classes, and my spouse was constantly occupied, yet I had no time to share the burden.*

There were issues unique to Chinese immigrant entrepreneurs during the pandemic that impacted their wellbeing. Primarily, businesses catering to Chinese international students or tourists experienced devastating declines. The cost of studying in the UK soared, with flight prices increasing to approximately five to ten times their usual rates due to a lack of supply. Moreover, a prevalent perception among prospective students and their families was that the UK was a COVID-19 hotspot, rendering the pursuit of education amidst such risks imprudent. Concurrently, the number of Chinese tourists diminished to near zero. Businesses offering services to international students, as well as restaurants and retailers catering to both Chinese students and tourists, suffered profound setbacks.

Chinese immigrant entrepreneurs in the UK also grappled with a dual sense of alienation that negatively affected their wellbeing. Many participants felt that they encountered scepticism from their fellow Chinese citizens while also facing potential bias from certain UK residents. In the UK, Chinese migrants were attacked and insulted as the 'Chinese virus'; in Mainland China, they were accused of '*spreading poison from a thousand miles away*' (Hawaii Chinese News, 2020) as exaggerated narratives on social media led to an aversion by mainland Chinese against immigrants returning home, with the latter being perceived as potential carriers of the virus. One participant expressed the anguish of being unable to return to China to bid farewell to their terminally ill mother. Even the relatives and friends advised them against returning, fearing potential contact with the virus.

Meanwhile, given the outbreak's origin in China, many participants expressed concerns about blame and discrimination. One shared, '*many have died here [in the UK], and I feared they might attribute the deaths to Chinese, leading to retaliation against us*'. Likewise, another commented, '*although*

I hadn't faced direct discrimination, the online reports of Chinese students being chased and attacked on the streets by locals deeply distressed me. I was genuinely concerned for the safety of my family'. As the pandemic surged wave after wave, the predicament of Chinese entrepreneurs intensified. With no control over the pandemic's course, they had no choice but to adapt and maintain a positive attitude towards life. The virus' ruthless impact had made some of them prioritise life and wellbeing even more.

Self-Care as a Means to Sustain and Improve Wellbeing

We found that Chinese immigrant entrepreneurs adopt a variety of strategies aimed at preserving and enhancing their state of wellbeing. Predominantly, these strategies are centred around fostering self-care and attending to the wellbeing of their immediate family members, rather than focusing on aspects of their entrepreneurial endeavours or engaging with external stakeholders like business partners or friends. This emphasis on 'caring for yourself' emerged rather unexpectedly, presenting a contradiction to the communal ethos of traditional Chinese culture, which typically values social interaction and mutual support (Gao et al., 2022).

Our data suggests that diet was a frequently mentioned aspect of self-care due to the deep-rooted Chinese culinary culture (Zhou et al., 2023). The participants prioritised flavourful and nutritious meals (Lin, 2020), deeming simple meals like sandwiches and cereals as unsatisfying. One participant stated that, '*every meal is carefully prepared, avoiding raw and cold food. Eating well leads to good physical and mental health*'. This emphasis on food was also extended to vegetable farming, with many families converting their gardens into vegetable patches for fresh produce year-round, which further benefited their wellbeing.

Negative coping mechanisms also existed in our data. There is a saying in the Chinese culture: '家丑不可外扬', which can be translated as 'family disgrace should not be aired publicly'. An accompanying phrase, '好事不出门，坏事传千里', which means 'good news stays home, while bad news travels afar', emphasises the importance placed on maintaining family pride. Consequently, when faced with excessive stress or emotional turmoil, some participants internalised their struggles. While younger entrepreneurs mentioned engaging in aerobic exercises, most were not fond of physical activity and therefore sought solace and consolation with their families. However, some could not articulate their emotions effectively, leading to bouts of irritability or moodiness. A female mentioned shedding tears in solitude as a means of emotional release, with such episodes occurring every few weeks.

While the significance of friendship in promoting wellbeing is noted (Liu et al., 2017), most participants (28) acknowledged the rarity of finding a confidant. Some tried to establish connections within the Chinese communities in the UK, yet their efforts were unsuccessful. '*It's difficult to find like-minded people*', many remarked, attributing this primarily to their busy schedules and the need to balance work and family. '*Who has time for many social interactions? Due to our hectic lives, we even sent one of the children back to China for grandparents to raise*'. While some discovered potential friendships within WeChat groups, the geographical separation made sustaining these relationships challenging. When queried about local neighbourhood friendships, they hesitated, indicating that locals, like them, lead insular lives. The commonality lies in both groups waiting for the other to take initiative. '*Perhaps both sides fear intruding upon the other*', a participant pondered.

Feelings of loneliness and isolation drove many to visit their homeland once or twice, annually, which stopped during the pandemic. Several participants mentioned that visiting family in China serves as an effective method to maintain good wellbeing as it not only alleviates being homesick but also helps validate their self-worth. One participant explained the cultural disparity, stating that '*while in the UK, one can have a comfortable life without significant achievements; in China, societal success and recognition are paramount, especially within the family context*'. This was echoed by another participant who said, '*parents and relatives all hope I can achieve great success and earn them 'face'*'. In Chinese culture, the concept of 'returning home in glory' is an important manifestation of 'filial piety' (Ren et al., 2022). It can even determine whether a child is acknowledged and accepted by their family. This explains the strong desire among many Chinese parents for their children to acquire quality (private, in the UK context) education, ascend the social ladder, and achieve career successes that they were unable to attain in their generation (Costigan et al., 2010). Meanwhile, young women are normally expected to marry promptly as a demonstration of 'filial piety' and may end up with unhappy marriages (Song & Li, 2023).

Many participants spoke about the need to be valued and receive affirmation from family and society, which influenced their entrepreneurial choices as well as their positive and negative wellbeing (Stephan et al., 2023). This desire for affirmation might be linked to an absence of spiritual beliefs. For instance, one female participant shared,

> *I never expected that a faith could have such a big impact on me. For the first time in my life, I feel inner peace. It's hard to believe how tangled and painful my life was for over 30 years before this.*

Despite the beneficial effects on their wellbeing, they often concealed their newfound faith from friends and family in China due to prevalent materialistic views and scepticism towards religion.

In discussing self-care strategies to improve and maintain wellbeing, they identified two main areas where the UK government and NGO support would be beneficial: firstly, accessible and professional entrepreneurship guidance in Chinese (Chen et al., 2019). Many entrepreneurs lacked awareness about specialised support leading to exhaustion since existing Chinese associations focus more on the elderly. Access to workshops or industry mentors could greatly ease their struggles. Secondly, an approachable and professional counselling on wellbeing, including mental health and self-care education. This would help not only the Chinese immigrant entrepreneurs but also their families and friends, creating a more supportive environment. The cultural concept of 'saving face' complicates open discussions about these issues. One entrepreneur's positive experience with a life coach highlighted the benefits of professional self-care guidance, leading to improved family wellbeing and personal fulfilment.

Conclusion

In the exploration of the wellbeing of Chinese immigrant entrepreneurs in the UK, several intriguing phenomena have been observed. These entrepreneurs appear to be in excellent condition, passionately engaging in their chosen ventures with resilience and dedication. Even amongst close friends, they rarely disclose any personal distress or emotional turmoil. However, certain poignant actions reveal hidden struggles, such as the agonising decision to send their young children to Mainland China taken care of by grandparents. These entrepreneurs harbour untold sorrows and challenges. While some try hard to adjust (Dimitratos et al., 2016), the majority find it difficult to integrate into British society and truly understand the local market. Even Chinese entrepreneurs educated in the UK feel that language is a significant barrier to assimilating into the local culture (Chen et al., 2019). Associating predominantly with individuals from one's ethnic group is a double-edged sword. It can offer psychological and resource-based support yet may also limit access to more diverse and potentially valuable resources which hinders entrepreneurial embeddedness (Wang & Warn, 2018). The UK government, following the example set by Australia, should extend enhanced informational support to immigrant entrepreneurs brought in through relaxed policy measures (You & Zhou, 2021). This support should encompass providing details about their ethnic communities and access to wider market intelligence, catering to the needs of these entrepreneurs who may possess varying levels of expertise.

The COVID-19 pandemic presents an extraordinary stressor, not just affecting business operations but also preventing reunions with family members in China due to travel restrictions and public opinion pressure. Reports on social media regarding '*Overseas Chinese returning home to spread the virus*' and '*Chinese individuals facing discrimination from UK residents*' have further subjected them to considerable mental anguish. Living between these two distressing narratives has been profoundly oppressive for many. However, Chinese immigrant entrepreneurs frequently endure hardships quietly. It can be suggested that a combination of language barriers and deep-rooted cultural norms together leads to their reluctance in discussing and seeking help for their wellbeing. Many find the concept of 'self-care' unfamiliar. Those conditioned to be 'filial' often continue to prioritise their parents' wellbeing over their own as adults (Ren et al., 2022). The concept of self-care is missing from their vocabulary, so any conversations about wellbeing are rendered irrelevant. Governmental and non-governmental organisations, while offering entrepreneurial assistance, should also provide specialised wellbeing guidance. This would enable Chinese entrepreneurs to become familiar with its significance and acquire skills related to managing their wellbeing effectively.

This chapter also validates immigrant entrepreneurs' wellbeing, which is gendered. If it is posited that most Chinese entrepreneurial figures are confined by the cultural shackle of 'filial piety', inhibiting their ability to adequately care for themselves, then Chinese female entrepreneurs bear an additional burden, that of the societal expectation of 'domestic femininity'. Despite the call for gender equality, these traditional beliefs remain entrenched in many Chinese families. Consequently, it appears they are facing a dilemma: being a strong, independent professional devoid of familial ties or catering to the family, forsaking personal aspirations (Song & Li, 2023). Chinese female entrepreneurs confront a broader spectrum of challenges and pressures in their entrepreneurial journey than their male counterparts. However, it cannot deny the UK provides more opportunities for women to engage in entrepreneurship and self-realisation. The resilience and determination they demonstrate in their endeavours are truly unparalleled, and more research studies on Chinese female immigrant entrepreneurs are needed to explore the complex interplay of cultural, social, and professional factors influencing their journey. Moreover, studying female immigrant entrepreneurship in different regions enables comparisons of destination countries' strategies, revealing those that best ensure long-term survival, which can guide host societies in creating policies to enhance these entrepreneurs' wellbeing.

References

Alrawadieh, Z., Altinay, L., Cetin, G., & Şimşek, D. (2021). The interface between hospitality and tourism entrepreneurship, integration and well-being: A study of refugee entrepreneurs. *International Journal of Hospitality Management*, *97*, 103013. https://doi.org/10.1016/j.ijhm.2021.103013

Bönte, W., & Piegeler, M. (2013). Gender gap in latent and nascent entrepreneurship: Driven by competitiveness. *Small Business Economics*, *41*, 961–987. https://doi.org/10.1007/s11187-012-9459-3

Brieger, S. A., & Gielnik, M. M. (2021). Understanding the gender gap in immigrant entrepreneurship: A multi-country study of immigrants' embeddedness in economic, social, and institutional contexts. *Small Business Economics*, *56*, 1007–1031. https://doi.org/10.1007/s11187-019-00314-x

CFE/DueDil. (2014). Migrant entrepreneurs: Building our businesses, creating our jobs. Centre for Entrepreneurs. https://centreforentrepreneurs.org/ cfe-research/creating-our-jobs/

CFE/DueDil. (2024). *Migrants behind one in seven UK companies.* Centre for Entrepreneurs. https://centreforentrepreneurs.org/releases/migrants-behind-one-in-seven-uk-companies/

Chaudhry, S., & Crick, D. (2004). The business practices of small Chinese restaurants in the UK: An exploratory investigation. *Strategic Change*, *13*(1), 37–49. https://doi.org/10.1002/jsc.655

Chen, W., Tabari, S., & Prokop, D. (2023). Survival instincts of Chinese entrepreneurs in the UK: Adaptation or hibernation. *International Journal of Entrepreneurship and Small Business*, *1*(1). https://doi.org/10.1504/ijesb.2025.10059695

Chen, W., Tajeddini, K., Ratten, V., & Tabari, S. (2019). Educational immigrants: Evidence from Chinese young entrepreneurs in the UK. *Journal of Enterprising Communities: People and Places in the Global Economy*, *13*(1/2), 196–215. https://doi.org/10.1108/JEC-11-2018-0093

Chen, W., Tan, J., & Tu, F. (2015). Minding the gender gap: Social network and internet correlates of business performance among Chinese immigrant entrepreneurs. *American Behavioral Scientist*, *59*(8), 977–991. https://doi-org/10.1177/0002764215580 60

Chreim, S., Spence, M., Crick, D., & Liao, X. (2018). Review of female immigrant entrepreneurship research: Past findings, gaps and ways forward. *European Management Journal*, *36*(2), 210–222. https://doi.org/10.1016/j.emj.2018.02.001

Collins, J., & Low, A. (2010). Asian female immigrant entrepreneurs in small and medium-sized businesses in Australia. *Entrepreneurship and Regional Development*, *22*(1), 97–111. https://doi.org/10.1080/08985620903220553

Contreras-Barraza, N., Espinosa-Cristia, J. F., Salazar-Sepulveda, G., Vega-Muñoz, A., & Ariza-Montes, A. (2021). A scientometric systematic review of entrepreneurial wellbeing knowledge production. *Frontiers in Psychology*, *12*, 641465. https://doi.org/10.3389/fpsyg.2021.641465

Costigan, C. L., Hua, J. M., & Su, T. F. (2010). Living up to expectations: The strengths and challenges experienced by Chinese Canadian students. *Canadian Journal of School Psychology*, *25*(3), 223–245. https://doi.org/10.1177/0829573510368941

Dheer, R. J. (2018). Entrepreneurship by immigrants: A review of existing literature and directions for future research. *International Entrepreneurship and Management Journal*, *14*, 555–614. https://doi.org/10.1007/s11365-018-0506-7

Diener, E., Suh, E. M., Lucas, R. E., & Smith, H. L. (1999). Subjective well-being: Three decades of progress. *Psychological Bulletin*, *125*(2), 276–302. https://doi.org/10.1037/0033-2909.125.2.276

Dimitratos, P., Buck, T., Fletcher, M., & Li, N. (2016). The motivation of international entrepreneurship: The case of Chinese transnational entrepreneurs. *International Business Review*, *25*(5), 1103–1113. https://doi.org/10.1016/j.ibusrev.2016.01.012

Gao, J., Chen, T., Schøtt, T., & Gu, F. (2022). Entrepreneurs' life satisfaction built on satisfaction with job and work–family balance: Embedded in society in China, Finland, and Sweden. *Sustainability*, *14*(9), 5721. https://doi.org/10.3390/su14095721

Gudkova, S. (2018). Interviewing in qualitative research. In M. Ciesielska & D. Jemielniak (Eds.), *Qualitative methodologies in organization studies*. Cham: Palgrave Macmillan. https://doi.org/10.1007/978-3-319-65442-3_4

Guerrero, M., Mandakovic, V., Apablaza, M., & Arriagada, V. (2021). Are migrants in/from emerging economies more entrepreneurial than natives?. *International Entrepreneurship and Management Journal*, *17*, 527–548. https://doi.org/10.1007/s11365-020-00714-6

Hack-Polay, D., Tenna Ogbaburu, J., Rahman, M., & Mahmoud, A. B. (2020). Immigrant entrepreneurs in rural England–An examination of the socio-cultural barriers facing migrant small businesses in Lincolnshire. *Local Economy*, *35*(7), 676–694. https://doi.org/10.1177/0269094220988852

Hawaii Chinese News. (2020, March 19). *The students are crying! Being beaten abroad and being called 'Chinese virus', returning to China was called 'poisoned thousands of miles'.* https://www.facebook.com/363636593659528/posts/3128006167222543/

Heilbrunn, S. (2004). Impact of gender on difficulties faced by entrepreneurs. *The International Journal of Entrepreneurship and Innovation*, *5*(3), 159–165. https://doi.org/10.5367/0000000041513420

HomeOffice. (2020). *Immigration statistics, year ending June 2020 second edition.* https://www.gov.uk/government/statistics/immigration-statistics-year-ending-june-2020

Jones, P., Maas, G., Dobson, S., Newbery, R., Agyapong, D., & Matlay, H. (2018). Entrepreneurship in Africa, part 2: Entrepreneurial education and eco-systems. *Journal of Small Business and Enterprise Development*, *25*(4), 550–553. https://doi.org/10.1108/JSBED-08-2018-400

Koellinger, P., Minniti, M., & Schade, C. (2013). Gender differences in entrepreneurial propensity. *Oxford Bulletin of Economics and Statistics*, *75*(2), 213–234. https://doi.org/10.1111/j.1468-0084.2011.00689.x

Lin, X. (2020). Yang sheng, care and changing family relations in China: About a 'left-behind' mother's diet. *Families, Relationships and Societies*, *9*(2), 287–301. https://doi.org/10.1332/204674318X15384073468565

Liu, H., Liang, Z., & Chunyu, M. D. (2023). Chinese immigrant entrepreneurship in the United States: Temporal and spatial dimensions. *Journal of Ethnic and Migration Studies*, *49*(11), 2855–2876. https://doi.org/10.1080/1369183X.2021.2007063

Liu, J., Guo, M., Xu, L., Mao, W., & Chi, I. (2017). Family relationships, social connections, and depressive symptoms among Chinese older adults in international migrant families. *Journal of Ethnic & Cultural Diversity in Social Work*, *26*(3), 167–184. https://doi.org/10.1080/15313204.2016.1206496

Malerba, R. C., & Ferreira, J. J. (2020). Immigrant entrepreneurship and strategy: A systematic literature review. *Journal of Small Business & Entrepreneurship*, *33*(2), 183–217. https://doi.org/10.1080/08276331.2020.1804714

Minniti, M., & Naudé, W. (2010). What do we know about the patterns and determinants of female entrepreneurship across countries? *The European Journal of Development Research*, *22*, 277–293. https://doi.org/10.1057/ejdr.2010.17

Muravyev, A., Talavera, O., & Schäfer, D. (2009). Entrepreneurs' gender and financial constraints: Evidence from international data. *Journal of Comparative Economics*, *37*(2), 270–286. https://doi.org/10.1016/j.jce.2008.12.001

Patrickson, M., & Hallo, L. (2021). Female immigrant entrepreneurship: The experience of Chinese migrants to Australia. *Administrative Sciences*, *11*(4), 145. https://doi.org/10.3390/admsci11040145

Poblete, C. (2018). Shaping the castle according to the rocks in the path? Perceived discrimination, social differences, and subjective wellbeing as determinants of firm type among immigrant entrepreneurs. *Journal of International Entrepreneurship*, *16*, 276–300. https://doi.org/10.1007/s10843-018-0224-9

Quan, R., Fan, M., Zhang, M., & Sun, H. (2019). A dynamic dual model: The determinants of transnational migrant entrepreneurs' embeddedness in the UK. *Journal of Entrepreneurship, Management and Innovation*, *15*(2), 29–56. https://doi.org/10.7341/20191522

Ren, P., Emiliussen, J., Christiansen, R., Engelsen, S., & Klausen, S. H. (2022). Filial piety, generativity and older adults' wellbeing and loneliness in Denmark and China. *Applied Research in Quality of Life*, *17*(5), 3069–3090. https://doi.org/10.1007/s11482-022-10053-z

Roberts, R., Ram, M., Jones, T., Idris, B., Hart, M., Ri, A., & Prashar, N. (2020). *Unlocking opportunity: The value of ethnic minority firms in UK economic activity and enterprise*. Blackpool: Federation of Small Businesses.

Rodríguez-Gutiérrez, M. J., Romero, I., & Yu, Z. (2020). Guanxi and risk-taking propensity in Chinese immigrants' businesses. *International Entrepreneurship and Management Journal*, *16*, 305–325. https://doi.org/10.1007/s11365-019-00566-9

Ryan, R. M., & Deci, E. L. (2001). On happiness and human potentials: A review of research on hedonic and eudaimonic well-being. *Annual Review of Psychology*, *52*(1), 141–166. https://doi.org/10.1146/annurev.psych.52.1.141

Saker-Clark, H. (2023, September 04). Research finds 'marked rise' in women starting firms to boost work-life balance. *The Independent*. https://www.independent.co.uk/news/uk/women-entrepreneurs-marked-rise-balance-b2404259.html

Sánchez-García, J. C., Vargas-Morúa, G., & Hernández-Sánchez, B. R. (2018). Entrepreneurs' well-being: A bibliometric review. *Frontiers in Psychology*, *9*, 1696. https://doi.org/10.3389/fpsyg.2018.01696

Sarihasan, I., Dajnoki, K., & Al-Dalahmeh, M. (2023). Immigrant entrepreneurship and gender dimensions: A systematic review. *Intangible Capital*, *19*(2), 110–130. https://doi.org/10.3926/ic.2079

Sevä, J. I., Vinberg, S., Nordenmark, M., & Strandh, M. (2016). Subjective well-being among the self-employed in Europe: Macroeconomy, gender and immigrant status. *Small Business Economics*, *46*, 239–253. http://doi.org/10.1007/s11187-015-9682-9

Song, J., & Li, L. (2023). Empowered in business or penalised in marriage: Experiences of single female entrepreneurs in China. *Work, Employment and Society*, *37*(1), 3–19. https://doi.org/10.1177/09500170211028737

Stephan, U. (2018). Entrepreneurs' mental health and well-being: A review and research agenda. *Academy of Management Perspectives*, *32*(3), 290–322. https://doi.org/10.5465/amp.2017.0001

Stephan, U., Li, J., & Qu, J. (2020). A fresh look at self-employment, stress and health: Accounting for self-selection, time and gender. *International Journal of Entrepreneurial Behaviour & Research*, *26*(5), 1133–1177. https://doi.org/10.1108/IJEBR-06-2019-0362

Stephan, U., Rauch, A., & Hatak, I. (2023). Happy entrepreneurs? Everywhere? A meta-analysis of entrepreneurship and wellbeing. *Entrepreneurship Theory and Practice*, *47*(2), 553–593. https://doi.org/10.1177/10422587211072799

Sun, S. B., & Fong, E. (2022). The role of human capital, race, gender, and culture on immigrant entrepreneurship in Hong Kong. *Journal of Small Business & Entrepreneurship*, *34*(4), 363–396. https://doi.org/10.1080/08276331.2021.1959177

Thébaud, S. (2010). Gender and entrepreneurship as a career choice: Do self-assessments of ability matter? *Social Psychology Quarterly*, *73*(3), 288–304. https://doi.org/10.1177/0190272510377882

The Entrepreneurs Network. (2023). *Brief Paper: The foreign-born founders building our fastest-growing businesses*. Centre for Entrepreneurs. https://static1.squarespace.com/static/58ed40453a04116f46e8d99b/t/64dfaaf6043cc10fe64c161f/1692379907258/Job+Creators+2023

Verheul, I., & Thurik, R. (2001). Start-up capital: "Does gender matter?" *Small Business Economics, 16*, 329–346. https://doi.org/10.1007/s11187-011-9334-7

Wach, D., Stephan, U., & Gorgievski, M. (2016). More than money: Developing an integrative multi-factorial measure of entrepreneurial success. *International Small Business Journal, 34*(8), 1098–1121. https://doi.org/10.1177/0266242615608469

Wadhwa, V., Saxenian, A., Rissing, B., & Gereffi, G. (2007, January). *America's new immigrant entrepreneurs: Part 1*. Duke Science, Technology & Innovation Paper No. 23. http://dx.doi.org/10.2139/ssrn.990152

Wagner, J. (2007). What a difference a Y makes—Female and male nascent entrepreneurs in Germany. *Small Business Economics, 28*(1), 1–21. https://doi.org/10.1007/s11187-005-0259-x

Wang, Y., & Warn, J. (2018). Chinese immigrant entrepreneurship: Embeddedness and the interaction of resources with the wider social and economic context. *International Small Business Journal: Researching Entrepreneurship, 36*(2), 131–148. https://doi.org/10.1177/0266242617726364

Wiklund, J., Nikolaev, B., Shir, N., Foo, M. D., & Bradley, S. (2019). Entrepreneurship and well-being: Past, present, and future. *Journal of Business Venturing, 34*(4), 579–588. https://doi.org/10.1016/j.jbusvent.2019.01.002

Wilson, F., Kickul, J., & Marlino, D. (2007). Gender, entrepreneurial self–efficacy, and entrepreneurial career intentions: Implications for entrepreneurship education. *Entrepreneurship Theory and Practice, 31*(3), 387–406. https://doi.org/10.1111/j.1540-6520.2007.00179.x

Wu, M. F. (2021). *Exploring critical issues faced by Chinese immigrant entrepreneurs in the UK.* (Publication No. 30276681). [Doctoral dissertation, University of Salford]. ProQuest Dissertations and Theses Global.

Xu, F., He, X., & Yang, X. (2021). A multilevel approach linking entrepreneurial contexts to subjective well-being: Evidence from rural Chinese entrepreneurs. *Journal of Happiness Studies, 22*, 1537–1561. http://doi.org/10.1007/s10902-020-00283-z

Xu, Z., & Jia, H. (2022). The influence of COVID-19 on entrepreneur's psychological well-being. *Frontiers in Psychology, 12*, 6409. https://doi.org/10.3389/fpsyg.2021.823542

Yasin, N., & Hafeez, K. (2023). Three waves of immigrant entrepreneurship: A cross-national comparative study. *Small Business Economics, 60*(3), 1281–1306. http://doi.org/10.1007/s11187-022-00656-z

You, T., & Zhou, M. (2021). Gender and transnational dynamics in immigrant entrepreneurship: A case study of Chinese-owned nail salons in New York City. *Journal of Chinese Overseas, 17*(2), 239–264. https://doi.org/10.1163/17932548-12341444

Zbierowski, P., Brzozowska, A., & Gojny-Zbierowska, M. (2019). Well-being of immigrant entrepreneurs in their entrepreneurial life. *European Management Studies, 17*(1), 212–238. https://doi.org/10.7172/1644-9584.81.10

Zhang, J. (2015). A preliminary study of barriers to bank financing of ethnic Chinese entrepreneurs in the UK. *Open Journal of Social Sciences, 3*(07), 105. https://doi.org/10.4236/jss.2015.37018

Zhou, S., Ding, X., & Leung, J. T. Y. (2023). Healthy aging at family mealtimes: Associations of clean cooking, protein intake, and dining together with mental health of Chinese older adults amid COVID-19 pandemic. *International Journal of Environmental Research and Public Health, 20*(3), 1672. https://doi.org/10.3390/ijerph20031672

3 Dynamics of Entrepreneurial Wellbeing Throughout the Venture's Stages

A Focus on Women Entrepreneurs

Albena Pergelova

Introduction

Recent advances in the entrepreneurship literature have pointed to the importance of wellbeing as an outcome measure of entrepreneurial activities (e.g, Wiklund et al., 2019; Nikolaev et al., 2023; Stephan et al., 2020). Although wellbeing has been extensively studied in disciplines such as psychology, sociology, and economics (Ryan & Deci, 2001; Ryff, 1989), it is still an emerging topic in entrepreneurship. Scholars have predominantly examined hedonic wellbeing (e.g., positive affect, happiness, and life satisfaction) and to a lesser extent eudaimonic wellbeing (e.g., personal growth and self-actualisation) (Nikolaev et al., 2019, 2020, 2023; Nikolova et al., 2023; Stephan et al., 2020). Research suggests that entrepreneurs experience better wellbeing compared to wage employees (e.g., Hessels et al., 2018; Nikolaev et al., 2022; Stephan, 2018; Stephan et al., 2020). However, there are trade-offs between the costs and benefits of self-employment, and business ownership, which is not a panacea for balancing work and family role responsibilities and for achieving wellbeing (Parasuraman & Simmers, 2001). Overall, research on entrepreneurial wellbeing to date presents two important gaps, which this study addresses.

Firstly, research on wellbeing and entrepreneurship has usually taken a static approach (e.g., the *state* of positive or negative emotions resulting from engagement with entrepreneurship at a certain point in time or the assessment of overall life / work satisfaction at that point in time), measuring and comparing different dimensions of wellbeing for entrepreneurs vs. wage employees or for different groups of entrepreneurs. Such an approach has yielded a body of important findings on the relationship between entrepreneurship and wellbeing, but it is limited in its ability to present the personal experiences and *dynamics* of wellbeing associated with the different entrepreneurial stages (and related challenges). Yet, wellbeing is not a static concept, not something

DOI: 10.4324/9781003412403-3

you achieve once and for all, and it necessitates a more dynamic approach. Indeed, Wiklund et al. (2019) call for conceptualising entrepreneurial well-being as subjective experience that changes throughout the venture's stages. Similarly, Shir et al. (2019) emphasise the need to understand the processes involved in new venture creation and the fulfilment of psychological needs and wellbeing throughout those processes. For instance, entrepreneurs' sense of autonomy (and the resulting impact on wellbeing) can change as the venture unfolds (Van Gelderen, 2016). Thus, in line with the need to pay more attention to the dynamic and changeability of entrepreneurial wellbeing over time (Stephan, 2018), the focus in this study is on understanding how wellbeing levels fluctuate as the venture progresses and what the major factors are that affect wellbeing throughout the entrepreneurial journey.

Secondly, the entrepreneurial wellbeing literature has provided only limited insights on the wellbeing of women entrepreneurs (e.g., Chatterjee et al., 2022; Seva et al., 2016). The limited extant research on the topic presents conflicting results, with some authors finding that self-employed men are more satisfied (Georgellis & Yusuf, 2016) and others reporting that self-employed women have higher wellbeing than self-employed men (Sevä et al., 2016). Against this background, the aim of the current research is to examine the experiences of women entrepreneurs and changes in their wellbeing as they move through different business stages of their ventures. Specifically, this chapter poses the following research question: *What factors impact women entrepreneurs' wellbeing and how do those factors differ throughout the stages of the entrepreneurial journey*? To understand women entrepreneurs' experiences, an interpretivist research approach is adopted with a focus on women entrepreneurs working in male-dominated industries. This chapter offers the following contributions. First, the study develops a dynamic model of wellbeing which highlights different factors impacting women entrepreneurs' wellbeing as their ventures progress from inception through growth and to maturity. As such, the research addresses calls in the literature to reflect the dynamic nature of entrepreneurial wellbeing over time (Shir et al., 2019; Stephan, 2018). Second, the study unravels several novel factors specific to women entrepreneurs that the literature has not addressed before. In this way, the chapter contributes to a better understanding of the entrepreneurial journey of women and the resulting effect on their wellbeing.

Entrepreneurship and Wellbeing: A Brief Review

Hedonic and Eudaimonic Wellbeing

Two theoretical approaches have been commonly applied to the study of entrepreneurial wellbeing: hedonic and eudaimonic wellbeing. In the hedonic approach, wellbeing is associated with positive affect, the absence of negative affect, and life satisfaction (Diener, 1984; Kahneman et al., 1999). The literature refers to this approach as happiness or *subjective wellbeing*. The eudaimonic approach, which has been termed *psychological wellbeing* (Ryff, 1989), emphasises psychological functioning and focuses on whether a person is living a fulfiling life It includes several dimensions: personal growth, autonomy, purpose in life, self-acceptance, mastery, and relationships with others (Ryff, 2019). In entrepreneurship literature, most studies use the hedonic approach, especially measures of life or work satisfaction (e.g., Baron et al., 2016; Binder & Coad, 2013; Sevä et al., 2016; Hessels et al., 2018). However, recent studies addressing the eudaimonic approach (e.g., Shir et al., 2019; Nikolaev et al., 2019) apply self-determination theory (SDT) to assess the effect of key aspects such as autonomy, competence, and relatedness on wellbeing (Ryan & Deci, 2000). In SDT, autonomy refers to the need to feel that peoples' actions are self-directed; competence refers to mastery and expertise, and relatedness refers to the need for connectedness with others (Ryan & Deci, 2001).

Differences in Wellbeing for Women Entrepreneurs

There is scant research on the wellbeing of women entrepreneurs. From a hedonic wellbeing perspective, in a large European data study, Sevä et al. (2016) reported higher life satisfaction for self-employed women *without* employees (but no gender difference for self-employed individuals with employees). Conversely, Georgellis and Yusuf (2016) found job satisfaction benefits for self-employed men persisted over the years, while this was not the case for women.

From a eudaimonic wellbeing perspective, Bhuiyan and Ivlevs (2019) report that women micro-borrowers gain satisfaction with their financial security and feelings of achievement in life (an important aspect of eudaimonic wellbeing). In their study context – micro-borrowers in rural Bangladesh – the authors thus concluded that such eudaimonic aspects can contribute to the subjective wellbeing of women, but their results also indicate high concern over debt repayment, which leads to reduced life satisfaction. In another developing economy context – women in rural India – Chatterjee et al. (2022) found that self-employment can bring a sense of direction and purpose for women in impoverished communities, but family and social support were crucial for achieving psychological wellbeing gains.

Method

Consistent with the need for a dynamic approach to wellbeing that reflects women entrepreneurs' social situatedness and experiences as their ventures unfold, this study employs an interpretivist research approach, specifically, a life history narrative to allow for women's voices and lived experiences to surface (Mallon & Cohen, 2001). In-depth semi-structured interviews allowed for participants' individual stories to emerge. A common set of questions included the motivations for venturing into entrepreneurship (including life experiences leading to the decision), challenges and satisfaction along the entrepreneurial path, growth strategies, and the impact of their businesses on other aspects of their life.

Context and Sample

Interviews were conducted with five women entrepreneurs in stereotypically "male" industries located in Western Canada. The sampling was theoretical, focusing on identifying exceptional cases for theoretical development. The women entrepreneurs in this study operated in the following industries: manufacturing products used in oil and gas operations, services for oil and gas companies, real estate development/engineering, and technology-based businesses. The entrepreneurs were at a similar life stage – married, most had children, all had work experience, and they have been dissatisfied with their previous experience, which led to a desire to start their own business.

The numerical underrepresentation of women in such male-dominated contexts has been described as a "stranger who intrudes upon an alien culture" (Kanter, 1977, p. 207), a situation that enhances boundaries and makes the underrepresented group feel subject to constrained expectations. This presents an interesting research context because women entrepreneurs in male-dominated industries usually face additional pressures and, thus, are likely confronted with added challenges to balance expectations for firm competitiveness with their needs for wellbeing. The competitive nature of those industries require strong business acumen and specialised technical knowledge, along with agility and adaptiveness to new developments. All of those factors can increase the feelings of self-actualisation and personal growth for entrepreneurs (i.e., their eudaimonic wellbeing). At the same time, the fast-paced, competitive nature of those industries and the feeling of being a "stranger in an alien culture" introduce additional stressors and pose challenges to hedonic wellbeing (e.g., positive affect and life satisfaction). Although hedonic and eudaimonic wellbeing are both part of the concept of wellbeing and as such are expected to be positively correlated, it is also recognised that they are distinctive dimensions that can even be opposed to one another (Ryff, 2019). This is so because striving for personal growth and realisation is a self-demanding approach in life, which can be at odds with feelings of contentment and pleasurable experiences. Therefore, this context presents a unique perspective to understand the complexities of entrepreneurial wellbeing.

Data Analysis

Interviews were transcribed verbatim and analysed inductively to form first-order codes, themes and conceptual categories emerging from the data (Corbin & Strauss, 2008; Gioia et al., 2013). Because the participants operated in knowledge-intensive industries with sometimes highly technical

Table 3.1 **Data structure**

First-order codes	*Second-order themes (theoretical categories)*	*Aggregate theoretical dimensions*
Statements about the desire to be their own boss, the unhappiness of their previous work, and the importance of decisional control	*Autonomy*	**Taking ownership of oneself and ones personal growth and well-being**
Statements about practices that depart from traditional industry norms, and the importance of creating practices and processes consistent with one's values	*Doing things differently*	
Statements about the excitement of new projects and how creative challenges are used as a growth path that leads to satisfaction	*Creative challenges*	
Statements about the realisation of the impact of work on their health, practices to balance their lives, and self-reflection on mental health	*Awareness of the need to "maintain sanity"*	
Statements about feelings of guilt from being away from children, practices to reduce feelings of guilt, and internal tensions	*"Mom guilt"*	**Tensions between entrepreneurial demands and family well-being**
Statements about feeling tired, working long hours, and ups and downs that impact (mental) health	*Burnout*	
Statements about the flexibility to be with their children; the peace of mind knowing they can stop working when they decide and attend to family matters if needed	*Flexibility*	
Statements about support received from spouse and its impact on well-being, negotiating spousal support, and joint family/business decisions	*Spousal support*	
Statements about the dissonance between industry norms and the way they want to operate, external pressure to conform which creates stress, and breaking away from norms	*Confronting traditional industry measures of success*	**Fending off externally imposed views and practices**
Statements about perceptions of what entrepreneurs "are supposed to be"; societally imposed ideas	*Rigid ideas of what an entrepreneur should be*	
Statements about the difficulties of financing a women-led venture in a male-dominated industry; impact of gendered interactions on business opportunities	*Gendered interactions*	

(*Continued*)

Table 3.1 (Continued)

First-order codes	*Second-order themes (theoretical categories)*	*Aggregate theoretical dimensions*
Statements about initiatives and practices that empower employees and increases their well-being and building good relationships with employees	*Concern for employees*	**Satisfaction from contributing to the well-being of others**
Statements about how their business models and practices make sure they contribute to the wellbeing of clients; pride from "happy customers"	*Helping clients*	
Statements about the importance of social impact, how the business model incorporates elements of social impact, and what they hope to achieve that can benefit society	*Working towards a positive social Impact*	

products / services, interviews were complemented with industry reports and internal company documents. This process ensured a good understanding of the industry environment in which the women entrepreneurs operated. This approach also helped put into perspective the narratives of the participants and shed light into their experiences.

To ensure internal validity, following inductive research procedures, we conducted line-by-line analysis and open coding of the data (Corbin & Strauss, 2008). The analysis proceeded with the identification of successively more abstract categories emerging from the data and ways in which the categories are related to one another (axial coding). This process resulted in four aggregate theoretical dimensions which reflected different categories of variables impacting entrepreneurial wellbeing. The summary of the data structure is presented in Table 3.1.

Findings

This section presents the findings from the study, organised around the four aggregate theoretical dimensions that emerged from the data analysis: (1) Taking ownership of oneself and one's personal growth and wellbeing; (2) Tensions between entrepreneurial demands and family wellbeing; (3) Fending off externally imposed views and practices; and (4) Satisfaction from contributing to the wellbeing of others. Because this study is concerned with the dynamics of wellbeing as the venture progresses, the findings also pay attention to which factors impact women entrepreneurs' wellbeing as their businesses develop. Figure 3.1 summarises how the different factors play out over the life of the venture.

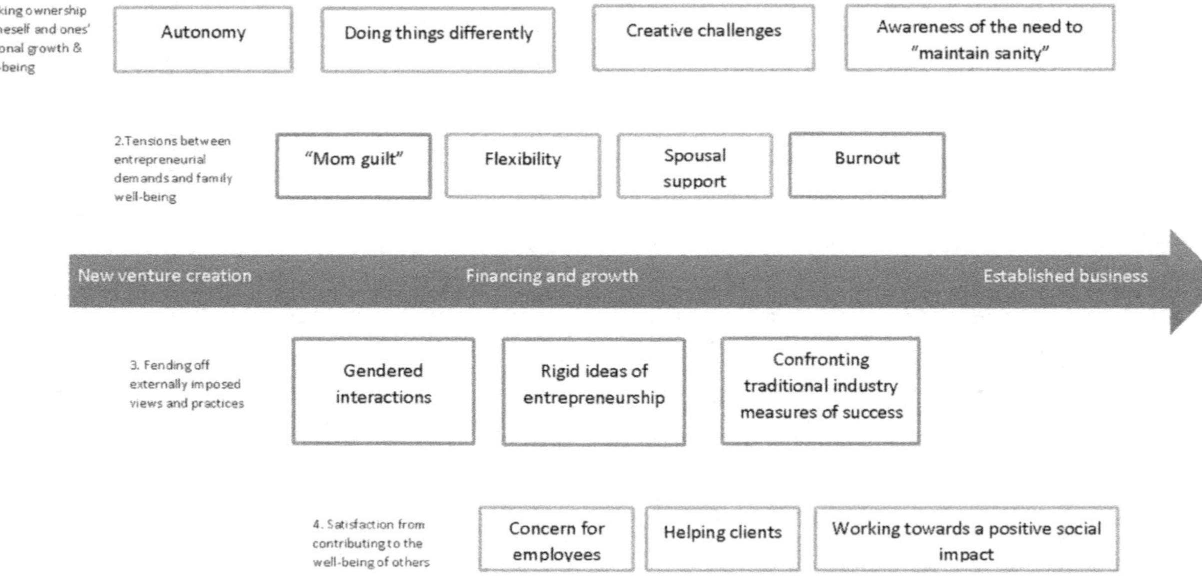

Figure 3.1 A dynamic model of entrepreneurial wellbeing (authors construction).

Taking Ownership of Oneself and Ones' Personal Growth and Wellbeing

This theoretical dimension underscores the importance of eudaimonic aspects of wellbeing that promote personal growth and fulfilment. It reflects the role of autonomy (both as a drive and as actualisation), departing from industry norms by doing things differently, dealing with creative challenges, and self-reflection to arrive at an understanding of the need to balance one's life and "maintain sanity."

Autonomy. At the beginning stages of the venture creation, the feelings of autonomy and the possibilities of fulfiling one's creative potential independently were a strong driving force and contributor to wellbeing. Autonomy has been identified as a critical motive for venturing into entrepreneurship (van Gelderen, 2016). However, Ryff (2019) and Ryan and Deci (2001) have pointed to the importance of differentiating between autonomy as a need (core motive) and the realisation of that need as a component of wellbeing. In this study, both aspects were clearly present. Dissatisfaction with previous work and life circumstances had planted the seeds for the need for autonomy. In the words of one participant: "*I was never good as an employee. I just always wanted to do more than I could as an employee*." Another one stated: "*I likened it to a race horse that's ready to race, but is being held back by the gate... that's how I felt for all those years, I was like 'I want to run my own business, I want to be my own boss'*." Venturing into entrepreneurship, thus, provided the women with an initial boost of satisfaction and wellbeing as they had the decisional freedom to organise their lives and careers. While the decision to start their own business was not taken lightly, the decisional freedom that came with it was the actualisation of autonomy for them:

> *And so, it was really extremely scary for me to do that, but once I had done it and started to reap the benefits. The benefits that I would never have ever received if I was someone's employee. First of all, and mostly, I am not answerable to "the man", and I say that because in all of the businesses I was in, I was always answerable to some "supreme man" along the chain of command.*

In line with Shir et al. (2019), the findings emphasise that acting in accord with one's own decisions leads entrepreneurs to experience greater wellbeing, especially at the early stages of the business.

Doing things differently. While autonomy is an important initial contributor to entrepreneurial wellbeing, it has also been recognised that there needs to be continuous efforts to maintain the entrepreneur's sense of decisional freedom so as to achieve continuous eudaimonia (Ryff, 2019). Thus, as the venture progresses and the initial "honeymoon" stage of euphoria from autonomy subsides, entrepreneurs' continued sense of wellbeing depended on their ability to self-organise in ways that maintain the commitment to the values that motivated their entry into entrepreneurship. In this study's context, this entailed re-evaluating the business models and practices as the venture started to grow and designing practices that depart from traditional industry norms and align with the entrepreneur's values. Participants shared examples of practices that depart from traditional business logic, for instance, one participant shared:

> *I found that in these planning stages, this kind of no man's land in between ... I'm kind of less satisfied, I feel really tired when I wake up in the morning. I'm a little bit more reluctant to start things, which is the reason why I have been trying to move projects forward when we don't necessarily have money for it. So, doing the social impact projects for example, those organisations don't have money to work with us, but if we can work with those projects and get that momentum going for those projects, I can still have that excitement about what we are making.*

This commitment to their values and the original idea that brought them into business was a meaningful contributor to the sense of wellbeing during the growth stages of the venture. Having the freedom to do things in their own way helped maintain momentum as the venture unfolds. As one participant expressed about her business practices: "*Not conventional, right? But I don't need to be.*"

Creative challenges. Another avenue for maintaining eudaimonic aspects of wellbeing as the venture unfolds was the response to creative challenges at work. Pressure at work was transformed into satisfaction by taking on challenges as a path to growth and enjoying the process. The *creative challenges* category thus reflected emotional responses to personal growth opportunities that combined fear and worries with excitement and satisfaction. One participant remarked: "*I'll be hopefully pitching it [the new offering] to companies like MGM, United Airlines, Home Depot and all sorts of organisations, which scares the hell out of me... [but] I feel way more successful now.*" Similarly, another participant said: "**it's a tough, tough project**. *But, it can also be used as a template for future developments ... so, yeah* **that's fun**." Characterising a situation as both tough and fun, scary and bringing a feeling of success, is an important aspect of eudaimonic wellbeing as overcoming challenges is used as a path to self-realisation. The study participants not only tolerated higher levels of stress but also used the stress as a stepping stone to increased wellbeing.

Awareness of the need to "maintain sanity". As the venture continues to develop in the stages following initial growth, women entrepreneurs were increasingly confronted with the realisation of the impact of work on their health and self-reflection on the need to balance their lives and health with the desires of building their company. Such self-reflections were important in order to not only maintain a positive affect and satisfaction with what they are doing (hedonic / evaluative wellbeing) but also reflect eudaimonic aspects of self-acceptance and the process of creating positive attitude towards the self and accepting one's current state (Ryff, 2019). Participants talked about the need to "*maintain sanity*" and the different practices they used in the process. One participant remarked: "*We all do the best we can, and we all have to get through life, figuring out how to meet our obligations, but, also, maintain some level of sanity and happiness while we're doing it.*"

The need to reflect on one's life and find balance was more pronounced once the venture was beyond the initial stages of creation and financing. At those later stages of the business, women entrepreneurs were consciously incorporating strategies to deal with the multiple demands in their lives as they were seeing the effects of long working hours and stress on their health and wellbeing.

Tensions between Entrepreneurial Demands and Family Wellbeing

Issues of work-family conflict and work-life balance have been widely studied by entrepreneurship scholars (e.g., Eddleston & Powell, 2012). However, the wellbeing literature has not explicitly studied the differential impact of the work-family interface for women entrepreneurs. The findings uncover important aspects of wellbeing that are being impacted by family dynamics and the crucial role that family plays for women entrepreneurs' wellbeing.

"Mom guilt". As they progress through the venture's life, women entrepreneurs are increasingly confronted with multiple dimensions that they have to balance and that significantly affect their wellbeing. One of the most vivid aspects affecting psychological wellbeing for our study participants was related to feelings of guilt from being away from the children, practices to reduce those feelings of guilt, and internal tensions arising from it. This need to balance the different pieces of one's life puzzle had "mom identity" at the core:

> *I think this is something that moms struggle with because you get the guilt, mom guilt sets in... 'How could you possibly want to be away from this beautiful, new born child that you just had', you know, it feels like or sounds like abandonment almost, I went through all those feelings of guilt...*

This "mom guilt" was a major factor and precursor to engaging in self-reflection and awareness of the need to maintain balance. Gendered socialisation and the perceived "moral obligations" and gendered roles that come with it seemed to have imprinted in women entrepreneurs the internal tensions that they were dealing with.

Flexibility. Interestingly, the "mom guilt" in some cases coexisted with feelings of peace of mind knowing that they can stop working when they decide to and attend to family matters if needed. This desire for flexibility has been found to be an important factor for women entering entrepreneurship. However, actually achieving flexibility can be complex for women who work in highly competitive, male-dominated industries. Even though there was a realisation that "*being the person who runs the company gives me flexibility to do that*," participants also admitted that

> *Often I am at conferences or I'll be there 12 hours a day. Like, often I have evening events, or networking events, or I have to travel. I try and keep the travel to an absolute minimum, but it absolutely occurs.*

Yet, as entrepreneurs were dealing with the multiple demands in their lives, they cherished the peace of mind that flexibility brings: "*And so now I'm free to make decisions that I can as a mother. So, if I want to be home after school to be with my children, I'm able to adjust my schedule to that.*" Flexibility, thus, counter-balances feelings of guilt and contributes positively to wellbeing.

Burnout. Feelings of burnout are common for entrepreneurs who work long hours even if they work on something they are passionate about (Baron et al., 2016). For women entrepreneurs, such burnouts impact both family dynamics and the entrepreneurs' mental and physical health. The beginning stages of the venture are especially challenging as one participant explained:

> *A lot of times [I was] working in my car and taking phone calls in the car cause you can't take them out on the street, because of sirens that go by, you can't take them in a coffee shop because of all the background noise, and you can't take them at home with the crying baby, so yeah, I was struggling and I felt desperate to get a good home base going.*

Importantly, for women entrepreneurs such burnouts can be more pronounced as they are compounded by multiple demands (family and business). For women in male-dominated industries, the mental load can be even heavier as they may feel subject to constrained expectations (Kanter, 1977). The desire to build a successful company in those industries while having and growing a family can build up stressors from external (industry) pressure and internal (self-imposed) expectations. In the words of one of the participants: "*The culture is that we're building the next big thing, we're going to make this huge company you know; speed is of the essence.*"

Spousal support. Support from the entrepreneur's spouse was an important component of the business/family interface that impacts wellbeing throughout the venture's development stages. The role of spousal support was evident both at the early stages and in later growth and expansion. Support could be moral, financial, or home and related to caring for children. In one of the cases, the participant explained: "*My husband is a stay-at-home father, he cannot get a job because we never know when I am working—it could be anytime.*" In another case, a participant shared: "*I've made some expensive mistakes and he [my husband] is like 'Oh well, we still have our house and we're still eating and we're still paying our mortgage'.*" Even with spousal support present, however, frictions can arise that affect both family dynamics and wellbeing.

The need to continuously negotiate spousal support can impact the levels of stress for women entrepreneurs, which ultimately affects their wellbeing.

Fending off Externally Imposed Views and Practices

Another critical component of wellbeing at the growth stage of the company was fending off imposed traditional ways of defining success and doing business vs. realising the women's own vision for the business.

Confronting traditional industry measures of success. Participants in the study expressed dissatisfaction with the pressure from traditional success measures and the way those measures conflict with their own understanding of success. One participant remarked:

> *A lot of people look at a business and think that if you're growing by numbers, either by the number of employees you have or by the amount of space you are occupying or by your financials or whatever, that means you are a success. I found that as all of those numbers went up, I was less happy. I was more stressed. I was more constricted in what I was able to do… I was losing sleep and I was really unhappy.*

Hegemonic discourses of economic rationality impose a view of entrepreneurial success that is limited and constrictive. For women embedded in a gendered field such as entrepreneurship (specifically, within male-typed industries), what counts as success based on the prevailing discourse can conflict with their own values and motivations. This leads to dissonance that they have to overcome as they search for meaning and wellbeing. Women entrepreneurs perceived aggressive industry practices / benchmarks as threatening their autonomy to decide what to do and the alignment with their values. Such externally imposed views of success were described by one of the participants as "*sucking my soul out of me*."

Rigid ideas of what an entrepreneur should be. In addition to confronting traditional ideas of success, women entrepreneurs had to reconnect with the ideal of the entrepreneur or the societally imposed view of what an entrepreneur is expected to be. In the words of one participant:

> *I've been very aggressive since then about learning all the time, advancing, having the proper mindset, having the proper understanding … I was torn in between this ideal of what an entrepreneur should be versus what my family needed. And I have to reconcile that.*

The women entrepreneurship literature has long advocated for a closer attention to the way the "heroic male entrepreneur" ideal impacts women's willingness to start a business (Jones, 2014). The findings point to the importance of attending to the way in which such ideals impact the wellbeing of women entrepreneurs as well. Rigid ideas of what an entrepreneur is supposed to be and do have deeply embedded roots and can have profound consequences for the ability of women entrepreneurs to achieve both hedonic (satisfaction, positive affect) and eudaimonic (self-acceptance, competence) aspects of wellbeing.

Gendered interactions. Externally imposed views on "ideal" entrepreneurs and ways of doing business were also evident in gendered interactions, especially at the stage of financing and growth. The entrepreneurship literature has provided evidence of differential treatment of women entrepreneurs when interacting with investors (e.g., Kanze et al., 2018), which negatively impacts women's business prospects. Such gendered interactions further impact women entrepreneurs' wellbeing. One participant explained:

> *The major challenge I'm facing right now is that investors tell me they won't invest unless I have a co-founder. Which is frustrating because I have very successfully run this business on my own for the past 3 years. So, they say they want a co-founder because essentially to share the burden of business. In saying that, they invest in a lot of single male founders, so, the only people that I have talked to for whom investors insist they need a co-founder, are female founders.*

Gendered assumption underpinning interactions (especially with investors and banks) have a major impact on wellbeing from both a hedonic and eudaimonic point of view. Being consistently told by investors that you are not sufficient not only can undermine the entrepreneurs' feeling of competence / mastery and self-worth, which is crucial for eudaimonic wellbeing (Ryff, 2019), but also can impact the extent to which entrepreneurs feel positive/negative affect and satisfaction (hedonic wellbeing).

Satisfaction from Contributing to the Wellbeing of Others

The entrepreneurship literature has established that women-led firms are more likely than men-led firms to pursue both economic and social objectives (Jennings & Brush, 2013). In this study, women were weaving social impact activities and objectives in their business models. While concern for the welfare of others and positive social impact was evident in the early stages, as their ventures stabilised after the first few years after inception, women entrepreneurs were increasingly striving to bring wellbeing for other stakeholders (e.g., employees, clients, and community). Thus, even though social aspects of the mission for their businesses were present early in the ventures' lives, the wellbeing related to it intensified as the venture unfolded and as entrepreneurs realised the impact they can have on employees and clients. The entrepreneurs' own wellbeing was thus enhanced by forging positive relationships and helping others.

Concern for employees. Caring for the wellbeing of employees was a major aspect of forging positive social connections that contributed to entrepreneurs' own wellbeing. One participant explained:

> *I'm supporting four households right now entirely, and that's a great feeling to be able to say that, you know if we keep doing these things, then we can just continue expanding, and I guess it's kind of like my business family, just keeps getting bigger and bigger and I love that part of it.*

The realisation of the impact they can have was a crucial driver for our study participants to undertake more activities related to employees' support in different aspects of their lives.

Helping clients. Another aspect of the process of building positive relationships with others that contribute to entrepreneurs' own sense of wellbeing was the business relationships with clients. Participants reflected on the way their businesses impact their clients and help them be stronger and more successful. The realisation that they can "*make life easier*" for others was a factor impacting positively their own life:

> *Through building tangible spaces that people live, and work, and exist in that brings them joy that they can't explain why, or how, or what caused it. So, I see it happen in [the co-working space] when people tell me that it's literally impacted their mental health to have a place to come work that's so warm, and friendly.*

Both treatments of eudaimonic wellbeing (Ryff, 2019) and SDT (Ryan & Deci, 2000) underscore the importance of relatedness and social belonging for psychological functioning and wellbeing. This aspect emphasises the fundamentally social nature of entrepreneurial pursuits and the need to build meaningful relationships with both clients and employees.

Working towards a positive social impact. Reflecting previous findings that women entrepreneurs tend to weave social features in their businesses more often than their male counterparts (Jennings & Brush, 2013), in this study participants expressed a desire to contribute to a positive social impact and the resulting satisfaction that this brings to them. Bringing the relatedness aspect of wellbeing to the local community and society more broadly, participants reflected on the significance that such social impact goals had not only for their businesses but for their self-realisation and feelings of achievement in life. One participant expressed:

> *We want to support the local content creators so that they don't have to move to the bigger cities to be able to have a career. But also, because we want to build those local creative economies. If you don't provide as a city, if you don't provide those local creative economies those creators will leave and then your city will not have the culture that it needs to be livable to the rest of the people there.*

Discussion

The findings from this study provide a contribution to the literature on entrepreneurial wellbeing and the women entrepreneurship literature by offering a dynamic model of entrepreneurial wellbeing that evolves over time (see Figure 3.1). The significance of wellbeing and the practices related to achieving it differ as women entrepreneurs move through the life of their ventures. While autonomy was a very important contributor to wellbeing at the initial stages of the business, women entrepreneurs had to find ways to maintain their feeling of decisional freedom as their ventures progressed by doing things differently, tackling creative challenges, and reflecting on the need to maintain balance in their lives. This finding aligns with research which suggests that the benefits of entrepreneurship for psychological wellbeing may change over time (Nikolaev et al., 2019). Indeed, the initial benefits can subside quickly if entrepreneurs are not able to manage the pressures that come at the growth stage.

An important part of the challenges that participants faced in maintaining wellbeing was found at the growth and financing stages where women entrepreneurs had to confront externally imposed ideas of entrepreneurial success and gendered interactions. At this stage as well, the role of family was pivotal in determining the wellbeing of women entrepreneurs. While "mom guilt" and burnout from juggling multiple demands can have a pronounced negative effect on wellbeing, spousal support and the feelings of flexibility can counterbalance this effect. Striving to provide wellbeing for others (clients and employees) was also a major contributor to entrepreneurs' feelings of relatedness and thus increased wellbeing, especially at later stages of the venture development when the business is more established.

The findings from this study highlight factors previously unexplored in the entrepreneurial wellbeing literature that can have a substantial impact on wellbeing and help shed light on the results of previous studies. For instance, Georgellis and Yusuf (2016) found that men entering self-employment will receive job satisfaction benefits, which persisted over the years, while for women transitioning into self-employment the increase in satisfaction was for the first year only. Our results confirm that an initial "honeymoon" stage lets women entrepreneurs experience autonomy, which provides a boost in satisfaction, but stresses and disillusionments can quickly tamper off the initial increase in satisfaction. Parasuraman and Simmers (2001) found that the juggling between work and family led to higher levels of life stress for women than men. Factors such as "mom guilt" and gendered interactions, identified in this study, can have a profound impact on women entrepreneurs' wellbeing in the growth stages of the venture. Another factor that has not received attention in the wellbeing literature is the need to fend off externally imposed views about "success" and what an entrepreneur is supposed to be. In this study, confronting such external norms occupied a major mental space in entrepreneurs' days and led to decisions and creative strategies that depart from the status quo. Successfully managing creative tensions and bringing awareness about the need to maintain balance and strategies to "maintain sanity" can help counteract the negative effects of external pressures.

The findings also highlight the important role of eudaimonic approaches to wellbeing. For instance, positive relations with others are considered to be a universally endorsed aspect of a good life and are a component of eudaimonic wellbeing, encompassing aspects such as having trusting ties to others, concerns about the welfare of others, and social relationships (Ryff, 2019). Previous research has found the importance of social functioning and relationships as a determinant of subjective wellbeing (Nikolaev et al., 2019; Ryan & Deci, 2000). In this study, contributing to the wellbeing of others (employees, clients, and society at large) and building positive relationships were important aspects that contribute to the wellbeing of women entrepreneurs. Another dimension of eudaimonic wellbeing that the findings highlight is self-acceptance (Ryff, 2019) or the ability to acknowledge multiple aspects of self and having a positive attitude toward the self. In the context of women entrepreneurs working in male-dominated industries, reconciling the multiple roles entrepreneurs played daily and finding ways to balance those "multiple selves" were a crucial element in the path to wellbeing. Overall, the findings join others in underscoring that entrepreneurial wellbeing should be examined via the dynamics of functioning well (Nikolaev et al., 2019), which includes autonomy, competence, relationships, and sense of purpose and self-acceptance. Entrepreneurial wellbeing cannot be understood fully by simply looking through a (static) hedonic aspects (e.g., feeling good/positive affect and satisfaction). The entrepreneurial journey is full of events that are challenging and require purposeful striving. While those may not always be conducive to hedonic wellbeing, they offer the opportunity to engage in building eudaimonic aspects of wellbeing and thus to be a fully functioning individual who embraces self-acceptance, personal growth, and purpose.

Limitations and Future Research Directions

While this study advances the knowledge on entrepreneurial wellbeing, it also presents some limitations which offer fruitful opportunities for future research. First, this study explored women entrepreneurs in male-typed industries such as oil and gas, high tech, and engineering. This context is particularly appropriate for examining different dimensions of wellbeing as it is fast-paced and demanding and as such, juxtaposes aspects of eudaimonic and hedonic wellbeing; however, women entrepreneurs in other industries may find that different dimensions of wellbeing are more prominent in their context. The extent to which the tensions identified in this study (e.g., "mom guilt," gendered interactions with investors, fending off externally imposed views of success) are applicable to women entrepreneurs in other industry contexts is open for further exploration. Additionally, the study participants were all opportunity-motivated entrepreneurs at a similar stage of life (married, with children, and with previous work experience in similar industries). Entrepreneurs at different life stages and / or necessity motivated might have different influences and perceptions about their entrepreneurial wellbeing. Finally, empirical testing of the impact of the factors identified in this study on wellbeing over time in future studies would provide invaluable insights about the relative importance of the different factors across time and address the needs at different stages for women entrepreneurs' wellbeing.

References

Baron, R. A., Franklin, R. J., & Hmieleski, K. M. (2016). Why entrepreneurs often experience low, not high, levels of stress: The joint effects of selection and psychological capital. *Journal of Management, 42*(3), 742–768.

Bhuiyan, M. F., & Ivlevs, A. (2019). Micro-entrepreneurship and subjective well-being: Evidence from rural Bangladesh. *Journal of Business Venturing, 34*(4), 625–645.

Binder, M., & Coad, A. (2013). Life satisfaction and self-employment: A matching approach. *Small Business Economics, 40,* 1009–1033.

Chatterjee, I., Shepherd, D. A., & Wincent, J. (2022). Women's entrepreneurship and well-being at the base of the pyramid. *Journal of Business Venturing, 37*(4), 106222.

Corbin, J., & Strauss, A. (2008). *Basics of qualitative research: Techniques and procedures for developing grounded theory*. 3rd ed. Thousand Oaks, CA: SAGE Publications.

Diener, E. (1984). Subjective well-being. *Psychological Bulletin, 95*(3), 542.

Eddleston, K., & Powell, G. (2012). Nurturing entrepreneurs' work–family balance: A gendered perspective. *Entrepreneurship Theory and Practice, 36*(3), 513–541.

Georgellis, Y., & Yusuf, A. (2016). Is becoming self-employed a panacea for job satisfaction? Longitudinal evidence from work to self-employment transitions. *Journal of Small Business Management, 54*(S1), 53–76.

Gioia, D. A., Corley, K. G., & Hamilton, A. L. (2013). Seeking qualitative rigor in inductive research: Notes on the gioia methodology. *Organizational Research Methods, 16*(1), 15–31.

Hessels, J., Arampatzi, E., van der Zwan, P., & Burger, M. (2018). Life satisfaction and self-employment in different types of occupations. *Applied Economics Letters, 25*(11), 734–740.

Jennings, J., & Brush, C. (2013). Research on women entrepreneurs: Challenges to (and from) the broader entrepreneurship literature? *Academy of Management Annals, 7*(1), 663–715.

Jones, S. (2014). Gendered discourses of entrepreneurship in UK higher education: The fictive entrepreneur and the fictive student. *International Small Business Journal, 32*(3), 237–258.

Kahneman, D., Diener, E., & Schwarz, N. (1999). *Well-being: Foundations of hedonic psychology*. New York: Russell Sage Foundation.

Kanter, R. M. (1977). *Men and women of the corporation*. New York: Basic Books.

Kanze, D., Huang, L., Conley, M. A., & Higgins, E. T. (2018). We ask men to win and women not to lose: Closing the gender gap in startup funding. *Academy of Management Journal, 61*(2). https://doi.org/10.5465/amj.2016.1215

Mallon, M., & Cohen, L. (2001). Time for a change? Women's accounts of the move from organizational careers to self-employment. *British Journal of Management, 12*(3), 217–230.

Nikolaev, B., Boudreaux, C. J., & Wood, M. (2019). Entrepreneurship and subjective well-being: The mediating role of psychological functioning. *Entrepreneurship Theory and Practice*. https://doi.org/10.1177/1042258719830314.

Nikolaev, B., Boudreaux, C. J., & Wood, M. (2020). Entrepreneurship and subjective well-being: The mediating role of psychological functioning. *Entrepreneurship Theory and Practice, 44*(3), 557–586.

Nikolova, M., Nikolaev, B., & Boudreaux, C. (2022). Being your own boss and bossing others: The moderating effect of managing others on work meaning and autonomy for the self-employed and employees. Small Business Economics. https://doi.org/10.1007/s11187-021-00597-z

Nikolaev, B., Lerman, M. P., Boudreaux, C. J., & Mueller, B. A. (2023). Self-employment and eudaimonic well-being: The mediating role of problem- and emotion-focused coping. *Entrepreneurship Theory and Practice, 47*(6), 2121–2154.

Nikolova, M., Nikolaev, B., & Boudreaux, C. (2023). Being your own boss and bossing others: The moderating effect of managing others on work meaning and autonomy for the self-employed and employees. *Small Business Economics, 60*, 463–483.

Parasuraman, S., & Simmers, C. A. (2001). Type of employment, work–family conflict and well-being: A comparative study. *Journal of Organizational Behavior, 22*(5), 551–568.

Ryan, R., & Deci, E. (2000). Self-determination theory and the facilitation of intrinsic motivation, social development, and well-being. *American Psychologist, 55*(1), 68–78.

Ryan, R. M., & Deci, E. L. (2001). On happiness and human potentials: A review of research on hedonic and eudaimonic well-being. *Annual Review of Psychology, 52*(1), 141–166.

Ryff, C. D. (1989). Happiness is everything, or is it? Explorations on the meaning of psychological well-being. *Journal of Personality and Social Psychology, 57*(6), 1069–1081.

Ryff, C. D. (2019). Entrepreneurship and eudaimonic well-being: Five venues for new science. *Journal of Business Venturing, 34*(4), 646–663.

Sevä, I. J., Vinberg, S., Nordenmark, M., & Strandh, M. (2016). Subjective well-being among the self-employed in Europe: Macroeconomy, gender and immigrant status. *Small Business Economics, 46*, 239–253.

Shir, N., Nikolaev, B., & Wincent, J. (2019). Entrepreneurship and well-being: The role of psychological autonomy, competence, and relatedness. *Journal of Business Venturing, 34*(5), 105875.

Stephan, U. (2018). Entrepreneurs' mental health and well-being: A review and research agenda. *Academy of Management Perspectives, 32*(3), 290–322.

Stephan, U., Tavares, S. M., Carvalho, H., Ramalho, J. J., Santos, S. C., & Van Veldhoven, M. (2020). Self-employment and eudaimonic well-being: Energized by meaning, enabled by societal legitimacy. *Journal of Business Venturing, 35*(6), 106047.

Van Gelderen, M. (2016). Entrepreneurial autonomy and its dynamics. *Applied Psychology: An International Review, 65*(3), 541–567.

Wiklund, J., Nikolaev, B., Shir, N., Foo, M.-D., & Bradley, S. (2019). Entrepreneurship and well-being: Past, present, and future. *Journal of Business Venturing, 34*, 579–588.

4 Belonging Nowhere and Everywhere

The Case of a Woman Health and Fitness Entrepreneur's Journey to Emotional Agility

Lizanne Gerber and Hannelize Jacobs

Introduction

The health and fitness industry plays a significant role in enhancing people's lives by helping clients achieve their health and fitness goals. Research shows that people who watch what they eat and stay fit experience better mental health and emotional wellbeing (Doan et al., 2022). Mental health and emotional wellbeing are interrelated concepts. Mental health involves your overall psychological wellbeing, while emotional wellbeing refers to your ability to handle and express your emotions (Keyes, 2002; Ryff, 1989). These are integral components of overall wellbeing, defined as a state of contentment, health, and happiness across social, emotional, mental, and physical domains (Sabitha & Rajeswari, 2024). Triggers, both mental and emotional, significantly influence individual wellbeing. Mental triggers stem from experiences that evoke negative thoughts, leading to psychological distress, while emotional triggers result from reactions to situations or people, often inducing feelings of sadness, fear, or anger (Goleman, 1996).

Keyes (2013) highlights that the absence of mental health problems does not necessarily indicate the presence of positive mental health, nor does the lack of positive mental health imply the existence of mental health issues. According to Keyes's (2013) findings, positive mental health encompasses two fundamental dimensions:

- "Feeling well," often characterised by a subjective sense of wellbeing, pleasure, happiness, or emotional contentment.
- "Doing well," which pertains to psychosocial functioning, meaningfulness, fulfilment, flourishing, psychological resilience, and experiencing flow.

Keyes (2013) integrates these dimensions of "feeling well" and "doing well" into a unified scale of positive mental health, defining high levels of this state as "flourishing," in contrast to "languishing," which denotes a lack of wellbeing.

DOI: 10.4324/9781003412403-4

Ryff (1989) and Keyes (1998, 2002) assert that wellbeing measures reflect an individual's assessment of their functioning in life (eudaimonic wellbeing), contrasting with hedonic wellbeing, where scholars focus on evaluating individuals' feelings about their lives. The primary distinction between the definitions of eudaimonic wellbeing and hedonic wellbeing therefore revolves around two essential constructs: feelings (toward life) and functioning (in life).

While many individuals feel good about their lives, achieving optimal functioning remains a challenge, necessitating a focus on eudaimonic wellbeing (Keyes & Annas, 2009). Personal growth, integral to eudaimonic wellbeing, correlates with self-acceptance, purpose in life, and positive relationships (Robitschek & Keyes, 2009).

Effective emotion regulation is crucial for emotional wellbeing (Park et al. 2022), with emotional agility enabling individuals to align their behaviour with values and intentions (David, 2016). Despite extensive research on wellbeing, entrepreneurial wellbeing remains relatively unexplored, particularly from a eudaimonic perspective (Shir & Ryff, 2022). Entrepreneurs in the health and fitness industry wield significant influence over clients' wellbeing but may also grapple with personal emotional challenges. This chapter presents a case study of a woman health and fitness entrepreneur as she navigates through an emotional battle, driven by a profound yearning to belong – a sentiment crucial for fostering a sense of life's significance and meaning. This narrative traces her journey from fragility to agility, set against the backdrop of eudaimonic emotional wellbeing.

This chapter unfolds with an exploration of foundational perspectives followed by a methodology detailing the case study's development. Subsequently, the case study of Sally is presented, elucidating key insights for women entrepreneurs. This chapter culminates in theoretical and empirical implications, proposing a framework for eudaimonic entrepreneurial emotional wellbeing and concluding reflections.

Conceptual Foundations of Eudaimonic Emotional Wellbeing in Women Entrepreneurs

Emotional Wellbeing

The concept of emotional wellbeing has been criticised for its vagueness and lack of unified operationalisations (Martela & Sheldon, 2019). Despite the absence of a single measure, Park et al. (2022) define emotional wellbeing as a multidimensional construct encompassing both experiential and reflective features. This includes how positively an individual feels about life in general, as well as judgements about life satisfaction, sense of meaning, and the pursuit of goals within cultural, circumstantial, and developmental contexts.

Eudaimonic Wellbeing

Ryff (1989) and Keyes (1998, 2002) are widely recognised as the primary contributors to the understanding of eudaimonic (subjective) wellbeing. They differentiate between eudaimonic wellbeing and hedonic wellbeing based on two main components: feelings about life (hedonic wellbeing) and overall life functioning (eudaimonic wellbeing).

Keyes and Annas (2009) emphasised the distinction between positive emotions and positive functioning. They argued that throughout life, emotions and functioning often coincide as individuals tend to experience positive emotions when their life is going well and negative emotions when they encounter difficulties. Consequently, scholars such as Ryff (1989) and Keyes (1989, 2002) suggest that measures of psychological wellbeing overlap with measures of emotional wellbeing, indicating that feeling good about life (hedonic wellbeing) and functioning effectively in life (eudaimonic wellbeing) are related, yet distinct aspects.

The model by Keyes's (2013) of mental health proposes a continuum ranging from flourishing to languishing mental health. Flourishing individuals exhibit high levels of both hedonic and eudaimonic wellbeing, indicating positive feelings about life and effective life functioning. In contrast, languishing individuals have low levels of both types of subjective wellbeing, indicating limited positive feelings and impaired life functioning. Individuals with moderate mental health exhibit either moderate levels of both hedonic and eudaimonic wellbeing or disparate combinations of each (e.g., high hedonic but low eudaimonic wellbeing or vice versa) (Keyes & Annas, 2009).

Historically, Western society prioritised hedonic wellbeing, equating happiness with pleasurable living (Ryff, 1989). However, contemporary perspectives increasingly recognise eudaimonic wellbeing, emphasising meaningful living alongside hedonic pursuits (Joshanloo et al., 2021).

Eudaimonic Wellbeing and the Sense of Belonging

The need to belong is a fundamental aspect of human wellbeing, contributing to psychological comfort throughout life (Lambert et al., 2013). A sense of belonging enhances one's sense of meaning and purpose, highlighting its significance in eudaimonic wellbeing. Although social relationships fulfil this need, Lambert et al. (2013) emphasise the subjective experience of fitting in as central to belonging.

Eudaimonic Wellbeing in Women Entrepreneurs

Stephan (2018) and Ryff (2019a, 2019b) underscore the necessity for research focusing on the eudaimonic aspects of wellbeing for entrepreneurs as this area remains less explored than hedonic wellbeing. This call for further investigation is echoed by Ryff (2019a, 2019b), Shepherd (2015), Stephan (2018), and Wiklund et al. (2019). Drawing on previous literature linking eudaimonia and health, research on entrepreneurial eudaimonic wellbeing identifies five key areas for future exploration: (1) examining the relationship between entrepreneurship and autonomy from both motivational (self-determination theory) and wellbeing (eudaimonic wellbeing theory) perspectives, (2) exploring the impact of different types of entrepreneurship (opportunity versus necessity) on eudaimonic wellbeing, (3) investigating eudaimonia throughout the entrepreneurial journey (from inception to conclusion), (4) exploring the relationship between entrepreneurship, wellbeing, and health, and (5) studying entrepreneurs' influence on the eudaimonia of others by contrasting virtuous and vicious types (Ryff, 2019a, 2019b).

Gender differences in eudaimonic wellbeing remain underexplored, with studies indicating more similarities than differences across genders (Joshanloo, 2020; Joshanloo & Jovanović, 2017). However, contextual factors such as gender inequality and traditional gender roles can influence women entrepreneurs' subjective wellbeing (Love et al., 2024). Women entrepreneurs in low-income countries may face greater challenges and report lower wellbeing than men, while those in high-income countries may experience higher wellbeing.

Emotional Agility for Eudaimonic Emotional Wellbeing in the Women Entrepreneurial Journey

Emotional agility is essential for navigating the dynamic challenges of entrepreneurship (David, 2016). It enables individuals to confront difficult emotions with courage and compassion, aligning their behaviours with their values and intentions. By accepting emotions and creating space between them and actions, emotionally agile individuals can adapt to stress, setbacks, and transitions while pursuing long-term goals (David, 2016).

Emotional Agility and the Women Entrepreneurial Journey

Entrepreneurship, as a self-organising endeavour, holds significant importance in contemporary society and profoundly influences individuals' personal growth, advancement, and overall wellbeing. Shir and Ryff (2022) introduce a dynamic perspective on the relationship between entrepreneurship and eudaimonic wellbeing, rooted in philosophical and psychological understandings of wellbeing's essence, as well as entrepreneurship's nature as a value-oriented form of empowerment. Utilising the action-phase model, they tailor it to the various stages of venture creation, including deliberation, planning, execution, and reflection. From this framework, they formulate key hypotheses concerning how core aspects of psychological wellbeing intersect with the entrepreneurial journey, considering different circumstances and contexts.

Emotional agility is a crucial skill for women entrepreneurs, allowing them to navigate the emotional rollercoaster of entrepreneurship (Matheson, 2024). As entrepreneurship involves unpredictable fluctuations between success and failure, emotional agility prepares individuals to cope with critical situations, maintain inner peace, and sustain their business ventures.

Methodology

This study utilises the case study method, widely used in academia by researchers interested in qualitative research (Baškarada, 2014). In a case study, real-time phenomena are explored within their natural context, acknowledging the significant influence of context (Kaarbo & Beasley, 1999).

For this case study, Rashid et al.'s (2019) four-phase approach was adopted:

This study adopts a relativist ontology, suggesting reality is socially constructed (Lincoln et al., 2011). Epistemologically, a subjectivist perspective is embraced, acknowledging the subjective interpretation of reality by both researcher and participant (Rashid et al., 2019). Qualitative methods were chosen to delve deeply into the phenomenon under investigation (Cresswell & Cresswell, 2017). The interpretive paradigm, rooted in relativist ontology and subjectivist epistemology, guided the study, allowing for the exploration of socially constructed meanings (Rashid et al., 2019). Abduction, bridging induction, and deduction were employed to understand the process of achieving emotional agility among women entrepreneurs (Järvensivu & Törnroos, 2010). Case study research was chosen due to its suitability for investigating real-life phenomena within specific contexts (Yin, 1994). Research questions were structured to explore real-life experiences rather than develop normative statements (Punch, 2005).

Research Questions

Primary and secondary research questions were formulated to guide the study, focusing on emotional wellbeing and entrepreneurial experiences (Yin, 1994).

The primary research question of the study is:

> How do women entrepreneurs achieve and sustain eudaimonic emotional wellbeing through practising emotional agility?

The authors employed a case study methodology, aligning with an interpretive stance and abductive research logic. This approach centred on the experiences of the respondent to elucidate the process of achieving emotional agility within the context of women entrepreneurship. The empirical material primarily consisted of semi-structured interview supplemented by participant observations, all digitally managed.

As qualitative research aims at interpretation rather than generalisation, reliability and generalisability were deemed irrelevant (Merriam, 1988). Instead, emphasis was placed on internal validity, focusing on the congruence of findings with reality.

Contact and Interaction

Empirical data was collected through an in-depth semi-structured interview and observation, allowing for triangulation (Yin, 2009). The participant's experiences were central to understanding eudaimonic emotional wellbeing challenges and emotional agility in the context of women entrepreneurship.

Case Study: A Health and Fitness Woman Entrepreneur's Journey to Eudaimonic Wellbeing

Sally's story begins with a deep love for sports and a desire to make a positive impact. Despite her humble background, she pursued education in biokinetics, unaware of the entrepreneurial path ahead. In 2006, Sally found herself at a local gym, not just training clients but guiding them in biokinetics for free. This sparked a realisation that there was more to her destiny. By 2008, she boldly positioned herself as a personal trainer and self-employed biokineticist, paving her path to success. Each day brought new challenges, but Sally's determination flourished with unwavering support. She embraced the thrill of entrepreneurship, realising her passion for autonomy and self-identity.

In 2017, Sally took a leap, establishing her own gym and introducing successful fitness bootcamps. Then, in 2019, she founded a health and wellness centre, offering a myriad of services and hosting transformation challenges that garnered hundreds of participants.

Sally's Journey from Emotional Fragility to Emotional Agility

Sally's journey from emotional fragility to emotional agility can be divided into five key themes reaffirming David's (2016) four steps for achieving emotional agility, namely (1) label your emotions, (2) accept your emotions, (3) view your emotions objectively, and (4) choose your values. The five themes from the case are presented in the following sections:

SECTION I: THE NEED TO BELONG

Sally's journey began with an unyielding desire to positively impact others, stemming from her upbringing and a deep-rooted need to belong. Despite the love and support of her adoptive parents, Sally's early days were overshadowed by the knowledge that her biological mother gave her up for adoption. This revelation fueled her quest for belonging and success, intertwining the two in her mind.

SECTION II: FROM SELF-DOUBT TO SELF-BELIEF

Entering the realm of entrepreneurship, Sally confronted self-doubt and fear. The stark disparity between her dreams of a conventional family life and the reality of her entrepreneurial journey weighed heavily on her. However, Sally's transformation began when she embraced the uniqueness of her path, finding solace in the understanding that her journey held its own purpose and value.

SECTION III: THE JOURNEY TOWARDS A NEW MINDSET AND MINDFUL LEADERSHIP

It was Sally's intense response to her need to belong and her feelings of emotional fragility that gave her the freedom to explore how she viewed herself and her entrepreneurial journey. Evident in Sally's pursuit to shift her perspective are the words of Maya Angelou: "You are free when you belong no place" (Brown, 2017, p. 8). Brown (2017) interpreted this as people often equate "belonging" with fitting in, but the reality is that belonging resides in one's heart. When we embrace ourselves and prioritise self-belief above all else, we discover that "we belong everywhere and nowhere" (Brown, 2017, p. 35). Brown adds that true belonging is not external. It cannot be found in people, places, society, culture, or communities because it resides within us.

In the initial years of her business, Sally grappled with a controlling leadership style, driven by her own insecurities. Her desire to belong often manifested as an obsession with controlling every aspect of her life, including her business. This inclination proved to be a barrier to personal growth and business expansion. Through introspection and mindfulness practices like meditation and journaling, Sally embarked on a journey of self-discovery. This newfound self-awareness liberated her from the constraints of control, paving the way for a more mindful and creative approach to leadership.

SECTION IV: NAVIGATING THE ENTREPRENEUR'S EMOTIONAL ROLLERCOASTER

Entrepreneurship proved to be a rollercoaster of emotions for Sally. Moments of stress and self-doubt punctuated her journey, challenging her resilience at every turn. Yet, it was through embracing vulnerability that Sally found strength. By opening up to her support network and expressing her fears without judgement, she cultivated deeper connections and emotional resilience.

SECTION V: STAY TRUE TO THE TRUTH

Through her journey, Sally discovered the intrinsic value of her experiences and the power of self-belief. No longer seeking validation from external sources, she embraced her entrepreneurial path as a platform for empowerment. Her perseverance through emotional turmoil has fostered emotional agility, enabling her to confront her vulnerabilities with grace and courage. Her entrepreneurial path is now defined by mindfulness, self-belief, and a deeper sense of purpose. Sally's journey underscores the profound connection between emotional wellbeing, belonging, and women entrepreneurship. Her story is a testament to the transformative power of emotional agility in navigating the challenges and opportunities of women in the entrepreneurial world.

Key Insights from Sally's Story for Women Entrepreneurs to Find Eudaimonic Emotional Wellbeing

Viewing entrepreneurship as a self-organising process suggests a direct correlation between an entrepreneur's eudaimonic emotional wellbeing and the phase of their entrepreneurial journey (Shir & Ryff, 2022). Shir (2015) outlined a fundamental action phase model of venture creation, comprising four distinct stages: (1) Envisioning and deliberation for potential entrepreneurs, (2) Planning and initiation for intended entrepreneurs, (3) Implementation for actively engaged entrepreneurs, and (4) Reflection and evaluation for owner-managers of established firms.

By integrating the self-organisational perspective of entrepreneurship with the action-phase model, Shir and Ryff (2022) allocated various aspects of entrepreneurial psychological wellbeing to each phase of entrepreneurial action: Phase 1 to 2 involves Purpose, Autonomy, and Positive Relations; Phase 2 to 3 encompasses Purpose, Autonomy, Positive Relations, and Environmental Mastery; Phase 3 to 4 includes Purpose, Autonomy, Positive Relations, Environmental Mastery, Personal Growth, and Self-Acceptance; and Phase 4 to 5 focuses on Autonomy, Personal Growth, and Self-Acceptance. The timeline of Sally's entrepreneurial journey is illustrated in the Figure 4.1.

Considering Sally's entrepreneurial journey timeline, it is evident that she is currently situated in the Reflection and Evaluation phase, which corresponds to the fifth phase of the action-phase model. Consequently, the

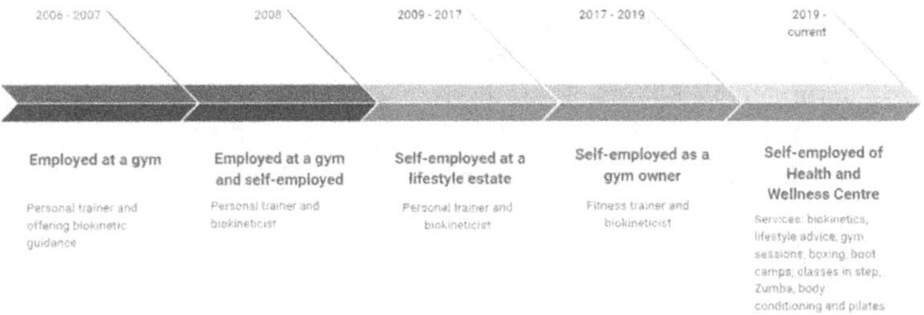

Figure 4.1 Timeline of Sally's entrepreneurial journey (author's construction).

eudaimonic psychological wellbeing elements that presently occupy her attention in this entrepreneurial phase include autonomy, personal growth, and self-acceptance. Remarkably, these aspects align with the key insights Sally has articulated for her fellow women entrepreneurs.

Key Insights

1. **Authenticity Matters but Isn't Everything:** While authenticity holds significance, not all successful entrepreneurs are exclusively defined by it. Remaining true to oneself can be a valuable asset, but it may not invariably be the sole determining factor for success in the competitive business world.
2. **Create Your Unique Stamp:** Excelling as an entrepreneur necessitates standing out in your chosen field. Merely conforming to the mainstream or offering conventional services is unlikely to lead to success. Identify your unique strengths, passions, and talents and seek opportunities to apply them uniquely in the market.
3. **Self-Exploration and Healing:** Before embarking on your entrepreneurial journey, invest time in self-exploration and healing. Understanding your true self, your values, and your potential is vital. Healing any emotional wounds and having faith in your capabilities are crucial for personal growth and business success.
4. **Develop Resilience:** Entrepreneurship often involves confronting criticism, setbacks, and challenges. Cultivating a resilient mindset fortified with confidence empowers you to discover your worth and strengths amidst complex circumstances.
5. **Strong Self-Image Is Essential:** Building a robust sense of self is not a mere cliché but a critical component of success. As an entrepreneur, you must believe in your worth and capabilities. A clear understanding of your

identity enables you to leverage your strengths, work on your weaknesses, and relate authentically to others.

6 **Continuous Self-Work:** Self-improvement and self-discovery are ongoing processes. The more you learn about yourself and evolve as a person, the better equipped you are to navigate the complexities of entrepreneurship. This journey is not finite but rather a continuous exploration of your potential.
7 **Resilience in Human Interactions:** Dealing with a diverse array of personalities and behaviours, especially in the entrepreneurial world, requires the development of resilience when handling criticism, negative comments, and rejection. Maintaining your authenticity while facing such challenges is pivotal for long-term success.
8 **Leadership through Authenticity:** Authenticity is not solely about personal wellbeing; it's also a pivotal trait for effective leadership. Being an authentic leader has the power to inspire and guide others. People are more likely to trust and follow a leader who remains genuine and true to themselves.

A Eudaimonic Entrepreneurial Emotional Wellbeing Framework: From Emotional Fragility to Emotional Agility

From the key insights from Sally's story above, a eudaimonic entrepreneurial emotional wellbeing framework has emerged (see Figure 4.2 below), charting the transformative journey from emotional fragility to emotional agility in the world of women entrepreneurship. Sally's experience highlights the power of personal growth and self-awareness as essential elements on the path to success and wellbeing.

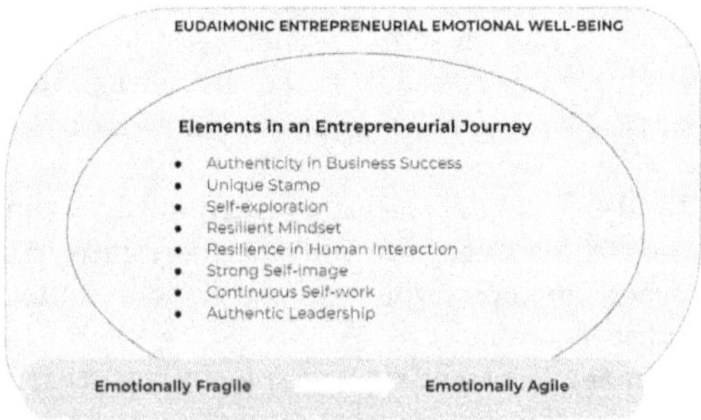

Figure 4.2 Eudaimonic entrepreneurial emotional wellbeing framework (authors' construction).

Conclusion

The narrative of Sally's journey from emotional fragility to emotional agility within the context of her health and fitness entrepreneurship encapsulates profound insights into the intersection of entrepreneurship, emotional wellbeing, and belonging. Rooted in the foundational philosophies of wellbeing advocated by scholars throughout history, Sally's story underscores the importance of eudaimonic emotional wellbeing in the entrepreneurial realm. As she navigates her entrepreneurial journey, Sally's transformation serves as a poignant illustration of the transformative power of embracing vulnerability, cultivating self-belief, and practising mindfulness.

The essence of belonging, a fundamental human need, resonates deeply throughout Sally's narrative, highlighting its intrinsic connection to meaning and purpose in life. Her journey underscores the significance of women entrepreneurs prioritising their emotional health, especially in industries like health and fitness, where they serve as role models for their clients.

Furthermore, Sally's narrative encourages further exploration into the eudaimonic emotional wellbeing of women entrepreneurs, emphasising the interconnectedness of emotional agility, entrepreneurship, belonging, and overall wellbeing. By delving into stories like Sally's researchers can glean invaluable insights to guide aspiring entrepreneurs on their quest for fulfilment and resilience in both personal and professional spheres. Ultimately, Sally's journey serves as a beacon of inspiration for women entrepreneurs and individuals alike, reminding us that emotional agility is not merely a destination but a continuous journey. As Brown (2017) aptly expressed, embracing oneself and prioritising self-belief illuminate the path to realising that we "belong nowhere and everywhere," navigating the complexities of entrepreneurship with grace and resilience.

References

Baškarada, S. (2014). Qualitative case study guidelines. Qualitative case studies guidelines. *The Qualitative Report, 19*(40), 1–25. https://doi.org/10.46743/2160-3715/2014.1008

Brown, B. (2017). *Braving the wilderness: The quest for true belonging and the courage to stand alone*. Random House. https://brenebrown.com/book/braving-the-wilderness/

Coffey, A., & Atkinson, P. (1996). *Making sense of qualitative data: Complementary research strategies*. Sage Publications, Inc. https://us.sagepub.com/en-us/nam/making-sense-of-qualitative-data/book5617

Creswell, J. W. (2013). Steps in conducting a scholarly mixed methods study. DBER Speaker Series. 48

Creswell, J. W., & Creswell, J. D. (2017). *Research design: Qualitative, quantitative, and mixed methods approaches* (6th ed.). Sage Publications, Inc. https://us.sagepub.com/en-us/nam/research-design/book270550

David, S. A. (2016). *Emotional agility: Get unstuck, embrace change, and thrive in work and life.* Avery. https://www.susandavid.com/book/

Doan, T., Ha, V., Strazdins, L., & Chateau, D. (2022). Healthy minds live in healthy bodies – Effect of physical health on mental health: Evidence from Australian longitudinal data. *Current Psychology, 2003*(42), 18702–18713. https://doi.org/10.1007/s12144-022-03053-7

Flick, U., von Kardorff, E., & Steinke, I. (2004). *A companion to qualitative research.* Sage Publications Ltd. https://books.google.co.za/books?id=6lwPkSo2XW8C&printsec=frontcover#v=onepage&q&f=false

Goleman, D. (1996). *Emotional intelligence: Why it can matter more than IQ.* Bloomsbury. https://www.goodreads.com/book/show/26329.Emotional_Intelligence

Gummesson, E. (2002). Relationship marketing and a new economy: It's time for de-programming. *Journal of Services Marketing, 16*(7), 585–589. https://doi.org/10.1108/08876040210447315

Hesse-Biber, S. N., & Leavy, P. (2010). *The practice of qualitative research* (6th ed.). Sage Publications, Inc. https://books.google.co.za/books?id=rkFaeLUsR4MC&printsec=frontcover#v=onepage&q&f=false

Järvensivu, T., & Törnroos, J. Å. (2010). Case study research with moderate constructionism: Conceptualization and practical illustration. *Industrial Marketing Management, 39*(1), 100–108. https://doi.org/10.1016/j.indmarman.2008.05.005

Joshanloo, M. (2020). The structure of the MHC-SF in a large American sample: Contributions of multidimensional scaling. *Journal of Mental Health, 29*(2), 139–143. https://doi.org/10.1080/09638237.2018.1466044

Joshanloo, M., & Jovanović, V. (2017). The factor structure of the mental health continuum-short form (MHC-SF) in Serbia: An evaluation using exploratory structural equation modeling. *Journal of Mental Health, 26*(6), 510–515. https://doi.org/10.1080/09638237.2016.1222058

Joshanloo, M., Van de Vliert, E., & Jose, P. E. (2021). Four fundamental distinctions in conceptions of wellbeing across cultures. In *The Palgrave handbook of positive education* (pp. 675–703). Cham: Springer International Publishing.

Kaarbo, J., & Beasley, R. K. (1999). A practical guide to the comparative case study method in political psychology. *Political Psychology, 20*(2), 369–391. https://www.jstor.org/stable/3792081

Keyes, C. L. M. (1998). Social well-being. *Social Psychology Quarterly, 61*(2), 121–140. https://doi.org/10.2307/2787065

Keyes, C. L. M. (2002). The mental health continuum: From languishing to flourishing in life. *Journal of Health and Social Behavior, 43*(2), 207–222. https://doi.org/10.2307/3090197

Keyes, C. L. M. (2013). Promoting and protecting positive mental health: Early and often throughout the lifespan. In C. L. M. Keyes (Ed.), *Mental well-being: International contributions to the study of positive mental health* (pp. 3–28). Springer. https://doi.org/10.1007/978-94-007-5195-8_1

Keyes, C. L. M., & Annas, J. (2009). Feeling good and functioning well: Distinctive concepts in ancient philosophy and contemporary science. *The Journal of Positive Psychology, 4*(3), 197–201. https://doi.org/10.1080/17439760902844228

Lambert, N. M., Stillman, T. F., Fincham, F. D., Hicks, J. A., Kamble, S., & Baumeister, R. F. (2013). To belong is to matter: Sense of belonging enhances meaning in life. *Personality and Social Psychology Bulletin, 39*(11), 1418–1427. https://doi.org/10.1177/0146167213499186

Lincoln, Y. S., Lynham, S. A., & Guba, E. G. (2011). Paradigmatic controversies, contradictions, and emerging confluences, revisited. *The Sage Handbook of Qualitative Research, 4*(2), 97–128.

Love, I., Nikolaev, B., & Dhakal, C. (2024). The well-being of women entrepreneurs: The role of gender inequality and gender roles. *Small Business Economics, 62*(1), 1–28. https://doi.org/10.1007/s11187-023-00769-z

Martela, F., & Sheldon, K. M. (2019). Clarifying the concept of well-being: Psychological need satisfaction as the common core connecting eudaimonic and subjective well-being. *Review of General Psychology, 23*(4), 458–474.

Matheson, K. (Host). (2024). Emotional agility. A must-have skill for entrepreneurs (Episode 125) [Audio podcast episode). In Unstoppable female entrepreneur with Kelsey Matheson. https://shows.acast.com/unstoppable-female-entrepreneurs/episodes/emotional-agility-a-must-have-skill-for-entrepreneurs

Merriam, S. B. (1988). *Case study research in education: A qualitative approach.* Jossey-Bass.

Park, Y., Kim, C., & Yoon, J. (2022). Exploring the relationship between an emotional experience with everyday products and its contribution to people's well-being and life satisfaction. *Affective and Pleasurable Design, 41*(41).

Punch, K. F. (2005). *Introduction to social research: Quantitative and qualitative approaches* (2nd ed.). Sage Publications. https://books.google.co.za/books?id=OvzPabc83HoC&printsec=frontcover&source=gbs_ge_summary_r&cad=0#v=onepage&q&f=false

Rashid, Y., Rashid, A., Warraich, M. A., Sabir, S. S., & Waseem, A. (2019). Case Study method: A step-by-step guide for business researchers. *International Journal of Qualitative Methods, 18*, 1–13. https://doi.org/10.1177/1609406919862424

Robitschek, C., & Keyes, C. L. (2009). Keyes's model of mental health with personal growth initiative as a parsimonious predictor. *Journal of Counseling Psychology*, 56(2), 321.

Ryff, C. D. (1989). Happiness is everything, or is it? Explorations on the meaning of psychological well-being. *Journal of Personality and Social Psychology, 57*(6), 1069–1081. https://doi.org/10.1037/0022-3514.57.6.1069

Ryff, C. D. (2019a). Entrepreneurship and eudaimonic well-being: Five venues for new science. *Journal of Business Venturing, 34*(4), 646–663. https://doi.org/10.1016/j.jbusvent.2018.09.003

Ryff, C. D. (2019b). Eudaimonic well-being and health: Mapping consequences of self-realization. In J. Vittersø & M. M. Tugade (Eds.), *Handbook of eudaimonic well-being* (pp. 205–220). Springer.

Sabitha, M., & Rajeswari, P. S. (2024). Holistic wellbeing in the workplace: Incorporating physical well-being for today's employees. *Humanities and Social Science Studies, 13*(1), 116–119. https://www.researchgate.net/publication/378774243_HOLISTIC_WELL-BEING_IN_THE_WORKPLACE_INCORPORATING_PHYSICAL_WELL-BEING_FOR_TODAY'S_EMPLOYEES

Shepherd, D. A. (2015). Party On! A call for entrepreneurship research that is more interactive, activity based, cognitively hot, compassionate, and prosocial. *Journal of Business Venturing, 30*(4), 489–507. https://doi.org/10.1016/j.jbusvent.2015.02.001

Shir, N. (2015). *Entrepreneurial well-being: The payoff structure of business creation.* (Publication No. 978-91-7258-960-5.) [Doctoral dissertation, Stockholm School of Economics]. ResearchGate.

Shir, N., & Ryff, C. D. (2022). Entrepreneurship, self-organization, and eudaimonic well-being: A dynamic approach. *Entrepreneurship Theory and Practice, 46*(6), 1658–1684. https://doi.org/10.1177/10422587211013798

Stephan, U. (2018). Entrepreneurs' mental health and well-being: A review and research agenda. *Academy of Management Perspectives, 32*(3), 290–322. https://doi.org/10.5465/amp.2017.0001

Wiklund, J., Nikolaev, B., Shir, N., Foo, M. D., & Bradley, S. (2019). Entrepreneurship and well-being: Past, present and future. *Journal of Business Venturing, 34(*4), 579–588. https://doi.org/10.1016/j.jbusvent.2019.01.002

Yin, R. K. (1994). Discovering the future of the case study method in evaluation research. *Evaluation Practice, 15*(3), 283–290. https://doi.org/10.1016/0886-1633(94)90023-X

Yin, R. K. (2009). How to do better case studies. In L. Bickman & D. J. Rog (Eds.), *The SAGE handbook of applied social research methods* (pp. 254–282). Sage Publications, Inc. https://doi.org/10.4135/9781483348858

5 Entrepreneurial Wellbeing of Nigerian Women Immigrant Entrepreneurs in Canada

An Intersectional Perspective

Wei Kang and Tolulope Oluwafemi

Introduction

The concept of wellbeing in entrepreneurship is multifaceted and often varies based on individual experiences and contexts (Diener, 1984). This chapter explores the subjective wellbeing of Nigerian women immigrant entrepreneurs (NWIE) in Canada, a unique group at the intersection of women entrepreneurship, immigrant entrepreneurship, and ethnic minority entrepreneurship. While wellbeing in entrepreneurship has been a subject of interest, immigrant entrepreneurs' subjective wellbeing remains underexplored (Amit & Litwin, 2010). This chapter aims to address this gap by providing insights into the wellbeing of NIWE, considering factors such as culture, faith, family, and entrepreneurship.

Background and Immigration Context

In Canada, an immigrant is defined as a person who is, or who has ever been, a landed immigrant or permanent resident. Such a person has been granted the right to live in Canada permanently by immigration authorities (Statistic Canada, 2023). Canada is recognised as a nation with a strong tradition of immigration. To respond to labour shortages due to its ageing population and declining birth rates, Canada's immigration policies have been strategically designed resulting in increased annual immigrant intake (Salami et al., 2020). Immigrant entrepreneurs play a crucial role in boosting the nation's economic growth. The inflow of immigrants has significantly contributed to the country's population growth, with over 1.3 million newcomers arriving between 2016 and 2021 (Immigration, Refugees and Citizenship Canada (IRCC), 2022). It is projected that immigrants will make up nearly 30% of Canada's population by 2036 (Ng & Gagnon, 2020) and immigrants from regions such as Asia, Latin

DOI: 10.4324/9781003412403-5

America, and Africa represent substantial portions of the immigrant population (Truong & Sweetman, 2018). In this chapter, we offer a deeper understanding of the experiences of immigrant entrepreneurs in Canada, particularly highlighting the challenges faced by women and ethnic minority entrepreneurs from diverse backgrounds. This understanding is crucial for shaping policies and initiatives that promote entrepreneurial wellbeing and contribute to the overall economic growth and prosperity of Canada (OECD, 2017).

Within the Canadian labour market, women especially from an ethnic minority group often encounter wage disparities and are overrepresented in lower-paying sectors (Block et al., 2019). Also, immigrants from Asia, Latin America, and Africa as well as ethnic minorities tend to experience higher unemployment rates than native-born Canadians (Ng & Gagnon, 2020). For many black and immigrant women, the propelling force to start a business is unfavourable traditional workforce conditions and even as black women entrepreneurs, they continue to face barriers, such as lack of encouragement, mentoring, sponsorship, and access to networks and information (Women Entrepreneurship Knowledge Hub, 2022). However, some female minorities find themselves pulled into entrepreneurship given positive factors that often relate to a desire for independence, recognition, and increased financial stability (Okeke-Ihejirika et al., 2023).

Nevertheless, entrepreneurship is a stressful endeavour considering all aspects of creating, leading, and managing a business (Cardon & Patel, 2015) and the additional "push" factors likely to impede black immigrant women from entrepreneurship. It is very important to gain insights into the experiences of NWIE, identify their entrepreneurial motivations and challenges, and understand what wellbeing means to this group, thereby aligning with the broader goal of shaping policies to enhance entrepreneurial wellbeing and stimulate economic growth.

Previous Literature and Definitions of Wellbeing

A comprehensive understanding of wellbeing is essential before exploring its intersection with entrepreneurship. Wellbeing is a multifaceted concept encompassing various dimensions of life satisfaction, happiness, and self-realisation. Within this chapter, we delve into the diverse perspectives on wellbeing, emphasising the need for a comprehensive approach to comprehend its intricacies. Two prominent perspectives on wellbeing, namely hedonic and eudaimonic, are particularly relevant to our exploration (Ryan & Deci, 2001; Ryff, 2017).

Hedonic wellbeing primarily pertains to the pursuit of happiness through the attainment of pleasure and the avoidance of pain. It encompasses three key components: life satisfaction, the presence of positive affect, and the absence of negative affect (Diener et al., 1999). Conversely, eudaimonic wellbeing delves deeper into concepts of meaning, self-realisation, and a person's degree of full functionality and vitality (Ryan & Deci, 2001; Ryff, 2017). This perspective on wellbeing is intricately linked to resilience and adaptability, particularly in adverse circumstances (Ryff, 2017). Eudaimonic wellbeing is rooted in endeavours that are self-determined and require substantial effort, encompassing a sense of thriving, authenticity, and feeling fully alive (Ryan & Deci, 2001; Ryff, 2017).

Subjective wellbeing theory highlights the deeply personal nature of wellbeing, shaped by individual interpretations of life circumstances. Within entrepreneurship, this subjectivity emphasises the need for a more nuanced approach to support the wellbeing of immigrant entrepreneurs, as stated by Diener (1984). Acknowledging the diverse experiences of immigrant entrepreneurs, considering elements like gender, ethnicity, and cultural backgrounds becomes crucial. Given the evolving global migration patterns and the rising role of entrepreneurship in immigrant integration and economic growth, it is vital to explore the interconnectedness of subjective wellbeing and entrepreneurial success. This understanding is fundamental for informed policymaking and comprehensive support systems. In this context, we focus on immigrant entrepreneurs, recognising that their distinctive experiences and perceptions of wellbeing are central to our investigation (Diener, 1984).

Wellbeing in the Context of Entrepreneurship

Entrepreneurial wellbeing, defined as "the experience of satisfaction, positive affect, infrequent negative affect, and psychological functioning in relation to developing, starting, growing, and running an entrepreneurial venture", offers a more direct and encompassing perspective on wellbeing in entrepreneurship (Shir, 2015). This definition includes psychological functioning aspects such as self-acceptance, personal growth, purpose, mental health, autonomy, and positive relations. It highlights that entrepreneurship can serve as a source of personal fulfilment, creativity, and meaning, embodying self-actualisation through purposeful, authentic, and self-organised activities (Benz & Frey, 2008; Block & Koellinger, 2009; Nikolaev et al., 2023; Uy et al., 2017). However, these measures might not fully capture the overall wellbeing individuals derived from engaging in entrepreneurial activities.

Immigrant entrepreneurship involves immigrants establishing businesses in a new country. This significantly impacts various aspects of immigrants' lives, such as economic success, social integration, and psychological adjustment (Amit & Litwin, 2010). Understanding the connection between immigrant entrepreneurship and wellbeing is crucial. Wellbeing greatly influences the drive, decision-making, and persistence of immigrant entrepreneurs (Stephan, 2018). This highlights the need for a comprehensive view of wellbeing among immigrant women entrepreneurs and a holistic approach which enriches existing literature and guides policies and support systems aiming to improve the wellbeing and success of immigrant entrepreneurs in Canada.

In the section to follow, analysis and findings from in-depth interviews with NWIE in Canada are presented. Through these findings, we gain a deeper understanding of how entrepreneurship intersects with wellbeing of NWIEs, highlighting the challenges and victories experienced by NWIEs in their pursuit of personal and professional fulfilment.

Data Collection and Analysis

We conducted two rounds of in-depth interviews with four NWIE in Canada in August and October 2023 respectively. The first round of interviews focused on the entrepreneurial motivations and challenges of the entrepreneurs. After the first round of interviews and initial review of data, we found some evidence that entrepreneurial motivation among this group of NWIEs was related to wellbeing (mostly eudaimonic), and the state of wellbeing of the NWIEs was also related to entrepreneurial actions and success. Furthermore, we realised that the unique challenges faced by this group highlighted the importance of wellbeing for the group. Therefore, we conducted a second round of interviews to explore the topic of subjective wellbeing among this group and to uncover the relationship between entrepreneurship and wellbeing for this group of entrepreneurs.

Data are presented using template analysis, a flexible style of thematic analysis (Brooks et al., 2015). Two *a priori* themes were created: entrepreneurship and wellbeing. Under each theme, subthemes were identified and discussed accordingly. We incorporated a lot of excerpts from the participants to offer a voice to women who often have limited opportunities to express themselves and share the truth of their experiences (Etter-Lewis, 1991). This approach aligns with our position on subjective wellbeing and provides a deeper understanding of the identities and experiences of this minority group (Essers, 2009). All four entrepreneurs interviewed are in their mid-30s, moved to Canada within the last six years, started their businesses in Canada, and all, except one, have other forms of paid employment. Additional demographic information about the study participants is provided in Table 5.1.

Findings

According to the interview guide and the *a priori* themes, two major themes were identified in this study. The first theme is entrepreneurship, and the other theme is wellbeing. Next, we discuss these themes and the emerging subthemes with excerpts from the participants for elaboration.

Entrepreneurship

Three subthemes emerged: about the venture; motivation; and challenges. We present our findings on each subtheme with excerpts below.

Table 5.1 Overview of participants

Participant name (Pseudonym)	*Type of business/ Type of entrepreneur*	*Academic qualification*	*Marital status*
Damola	Fashion: Manufacturing and selling ready-to-wear kids clothes made with African fabrics (Part-time entrepreneur)	MSc and other professional certifications	Married with two kids
Yemi	Food: Cooking and selling Nigerian meals (part-time entrepreneur)	MSc and other professional certification	Divorced/ no kids
Martha	Fashion: Sewing made-to-order clothes with African fabrics for adults (part-time entrepreneur)	MSc and other professional certification	Married with two kids
Layo	Information Technology: Technology consultant on HR systems (full-time entrepreneur)	BSc and other professional certifications	Married with two kids

About the Venture

The women we interviewed shared details about their business ventures such as the type of product or service offered, date of creation, mode of operation, and current status of the business. All four women operate in different industries including fashion, technology, and food. Two of the women started their business during the COVID-19 pandemic, while the other two started their business after the pandemic. Three entrepreneurs (Damola, Yemi, and Martha) operate sole proprietorships, while Layo operates her business as an incorporation.

Damola's venture is about kids' native clothing, and she described it as a business that is in the very early stages (established in 2023) with a lot of potential. Damola believes that business success depends on the ability of the venture to deliver a great product regardless of the entrepreneur's gender or nationality. However, she stated that being a Nigerian may have granted her access to certain fashion brands which she recognised as an opportunity that may not be readily available to other entrepreneurs in the fashion industry.

Yemi started her food/cooking business in 2020 after she was laid off from work during COVID-19 pandemic. Martha also started her fashion business during the pandemic due to the free time she had during the lockdown. According to Martha:

> *We make made-to-order clothing for women from ages 22–55 and for little kids. Our target customers are women of African descent and Caribbean*

> *descent who use fashion as a form of expression and like custom made clothes.*

While Damola, Yemi, and Martha seem to have embraced and converted their passions and local skills into business ventures, Layo's business is different. She is an independent consultant on the HR system. Layo worked in this industry while in Nigeria and upon relocating to Canada, she realised that she had to register a company if she wanted to continue in that career, so she took the opportunity to do so.

Motivation

Various factors motivated the women to start their business ventures including the need for self-fulfilment and happiness, financial stability, and the desire to connect to Nigerian roots; promote African culture; and add value to the lives of other African immigrants.

Damola recalled:

> *Whenever I go to my son's school, I see people from different Cultures, and they're not shy to wear their traditional attire. I wanted that for my kids..., to be proud of their African heritage and to know more about their Nigerian culture. I gave birth to my kids in the UK and then we moved to Canada, and they have never travelled to Nigeria.*

For Yemi whose hobby is cooking, she said "*cooking is a hobby for me, I love to do it and it contributes to my overall happiness. It is not about the money it's more about how it elevates my spirit and gives me a great sense of fulfilment*".

Describing why she started her business, Layo reflected,

> *I do not want to be this person that just lived for herself and her immediate family. I want to be someone who made impact. The greatest legacy I can give my children is not money or properties. It is the impact that I've made beyond my immediate environment.*

Describing her business, Martha commented:

> *I always like to see [African] women feel confident and beautiful in their skin, and it gives me great joy when I see someone wearing a piece of clothing I made, I smile with satisfaction. My business is also a way to promote African culture. Sewing is therapy for me. When I am on that machine, I derive joy knowing that I am creative and that I have a skill that I can offer to people. It's not just about the money, it's about making a change. My business is the vision I have. It is what gives me purpose.*

Martha further reflected on how women in particular feel the pressure to start entrepreneurship to contribute to household finances and feel validated by society. She said:

> *As women, (and maybe I'll speak for myself), we seek validation, we want to matter, we want to bring in finances to the household, and want to contribute to society in a way that we feel justified.*

We found that having free time during the pandemic lockdown and support from family and government, possessing local skills, hobbies, and passion facilitated the entrepreneurial process for these women. Two of the participants were able to start the business during the pandemic because they had the time to do so. All the participants spoke about the support received from parents and their spouses when starting out the business venture. Furthermore, all the women recognised that the "Canadian environment" is conducive to start and run a business. For example, Damola described the Canadian government supports available in the following recollection:

> *There are many support opportunities out here for business owners…, the government support is better here compared to the UK. When I moved to Canada, I was getting regular childcare support even though my husband and I have fulltime jobs. There are different funding opportunities I can apply to as a minority group or as a woman. [*In Canada*], business owners thrive, and the environment is favourable for them.*

The type of businesses created by these women are mostly from local skills and hobbies obtained and nurtured in Nigeria while growing up. These skills and hobbies, combined with the favourable entrepreneurial environment in Canada, presented opportunities for these women to start their businesses.

Challenges

The participants described some challenges they face in running their businesses including limited financial resources; hectic schedule; fear of the unknown and/or failure; access to local materials; varying customer needs; and unfavourable government policies.

In relation to funds, all participants (except Layo) commented on the limited funds available for their business, which is the reason the entrepreneurs keep other forms of employment and operate the business on a part-time basis. Reflecting on her inability to expand her business or quit her other job, Yemi commented:

> *Funding is my greatest challenge. I use the salary from my full-time job to run the business, so I can't just walk away from my job. Having my own commercial kitchen will require a lot of funds, which I do not have.*

Similarly, Martha reflected: "*funding is a problem. If I had funds, I'll be happy to expand my business and contribute more to the society*". Martha also commented that the issue of funding support is more critical for women entrepreneurs than men because of additional family and caregiving responsibilities a lot of women assume. In particular, Martha said:

> *As a female immigrant running a business, I feel more should be done to provide funds specific to our gender. For men, it is very easy for them to run a business they have more opportunities to thrive in their businesses than we do because of the roles we (women) must bear. They could just leave their family, work for 12 straight hours and when they go home, everything is ready for them. The kids are fed and bathed; the wife has cooked dinner. But if you were to put a woman in those shoes, the woman must face the challenge of cooking and other home management duties whilst also running a business.*

For Damola, while she didn't particularly mention funding as a challenge, she reflected on the uncertainty involved in creating a business which makes the entrepreneur cautious about how much money to invest in the business. She commented:

> *...for me it is not fear..., but it's just the uncertainty of starting something new. I want to invest as much funds as possible in the business, but at the same time I'm being cautious.*

We found that although all four women knew about government grants and funding opportunities available to support black women entrepreneurs, none of the women had applied to any of these grants. Yemi commented: "*I know about some grant opportunities, but I don't think my business is ready to apply for a grant*". Similarly, Damola commented: "*... I have been unable to apply for grants as a new business owner, but I will look into it*".

Although we found that having another source of income helps the entrepreneurs maintain financial stability, we also found that it creates another problem which is stress and hectic schedules, leaving the women with little or no time for other aspects of their lives. To resolve this, some of the women have simply accepted that being an entrepreneur is a stressful endeavour. For some, their passion keeps them going, while for others, they are gracious to themselves, doing the best they can and leaving the rest alone. For example, Martha reflected:

> *Starting a business is not easy but the vision for my business keeps me grounded. A few other entrepreneurial women I have spoken to also talk about how stressful it is. You really need to be strong willed to actually follow it through. You'll disappoint people, and people are going to*

disappoint you; goods are not going to arrive on time, you would lose money, you wouldn't make as much profit as you think you would make.

Although the women commented on how available services and facilities in Canada (e.g., power and internet) has helped their business creation and growth, they complained about access to the local raw materials which are either too expensive in Canada or unavailable. Unfortunately, international shipping policies in Canada do not seem favourable to these entrepreneurs. Reflecting on this issue, Martha said:

Here in Canada, I don't have access to cheap resources like I used to get in Nigeria. Things are more expensive here and shipping policies wouldn't make it easy for me to ship my fabrics. There's been a lot of culture shock and culture shifts for me in my journey to run a business in Canada. The business climate is very different and the resources I need to run my business are not easily accessible.

Another unfavourable government policy identified by Layo is the inability of entrepreneurs to contribute to employment insurance. According to Layo:

Entrepreneurs that own businesses and have about 50% or more shares in the business are not able to contribute to employment insurance in Canada. But there might be times when you would need employment insurance. For example, when a contract ends and you're not able to get another contract. I think this puts pressure on people to do multiple jobs such that if one contract ends, they have something else to fall back on.

Wellbeing

Three subthemes emerged: description and meaning; attributes and influences; and challenges and maintenance. We present our findings on each subtheme with excerpts below.

Description

All the participants converge in their description of wellbeing as a multifaceted concept. Generally, the women described wellbeing in terms of physical health, marriage and family health, social connections, and financial health. Damola commented:

Wellbeing to everyone means different things, for me wellbeing is connecting with my family, connecting with my children, spending time with my loved ones, taking care of myself, eating well, exercising, and taking breaks as needed.

Similarly, Martha reflected, *"for me, wellbeing is my state of mind. It's emotional, its spiritual, it's health wise and social".* According to Layo, *"wellbeing for me means every aspect of one's life is good in terms of health, finances, emotional being, mental being, spiritual and social".*

Describing wellbeing, Yemi commented:

> *Wellbeing ... is health related... not just the physical health but also emotional health, financial health and relationships. It is ensuring that you are in top shape and catered for emotionally, socially and financially because when one part suffers, every other part will also suffer. So, it's having an all-round "okay" status when it comes to all the metrics of your health.*

Attributes and Influences. The women attributed wellbeing to various factors including family and social connections; entrepreneurship; and flexible work arrangement. For example, Damola commented:

> *The number one factor in my wellbeing would be my family. Right now, my marriage is in better state, we are all healthy. If my family is thriving, if there's peace, if there are no challenges with my children, ... If my parents are okay, my siblings are okay, I think that automatically puts me in a state of good wellbeing...*

Damola further commented, "*Social factors influence my wellbeing, like the community I'm building, the people I get to meet, ... and being in a good work environment. I've been lucky to work with fantastic people*".

Two of the women (Yemi and Damola) who are part-time entrepreneurs described how hybrid mode of working in their other paid employment gives them time to do their business and manage their life affairs better. According to Damola:

> *Another factor that has influenced my wellbeing is good work-life balance. I get to work hybrid. Some days I'm working at home, some days I'm working in the office. I have deadlines, but I'm not tied down by strict schedules and that helps my wellbeing.*

Describing how working from home created time which she could spend on managing her business venture, Yemi commented, "*It was also easier [to run my business] because I was working from home 100%. My full-time employer didn't need me in person".*

For Layo who is a full-time entrepreneur and works from home, she described how this mode of working gives her the chance to achieve work-life balance. She reflected:

> *I work from home. I don't have to work long hours, so I have time to do other things that I love to do. I have time to practise my faith, time to spend*

time with family, and there is no need to pay for after school care since I am home when my kids return from school, we get to play together, bond and do other things.

The women described how the creation of their business ventures has contributed to their financial stability, happiness, and sense of fulfilment. Yemi commented, "*I think being an entrepreneur made me happier because I could control my time… I was happy and I was making more [money] from the business than my paycheck from my full-time job*".

Layo reflected:

I would not want my business to be taken away from me. It would really affect me because I've always wanted to own something that I'm proud of, and impact people and organisations with. My business brings a lot of fulfilments in more ways than one. So, if it's taken away, it's going to be a major setback for me.

Damola described how her business turned her dream into reality and gave her a feeling of fulfilment. She commented:

I feel 100% satisfied with my business because it's like turning a dream into reality. I wanted my kids to have a connection to their culture, their African roots and so, producing African clothing for them that gives them that sense of connection is more than enough for me no matter how much turnover I have. If the business is not profitable, I don't see myself as a failure. It only gives me a clearer direction of where next to focus my efforts… I see it as a learning opportunity because I am someone that enjoys the process more than the results.

Similarly, Martha commented:

To be honest, my business makes me feel good. I feel like my business has a purpose in my community and in my work in this world. It is what gives me purpose. There's a feel-good feeling I get from providing services to other people. The contentment and personal growth I experience… I think I would attribute to my business and the kids. If I weren't running this business, I would worry and feel underutilised. I like being busy, you really don't have time for all those other petty issues to gossip or be angry.

All the women acknowledged that the funds generated from their business contribute to their financial stability. Describing how this influences her wellbeing, Layo stated:

The financial stability I get from my business contributes greatly to my wellbeing. I can charge some utilities or travels to my business as an expense because I work from home. With financial stability comes peace of mind. I can afford my basic needs in life.

Challenges and Maintenance

The women described challenges to their wellbeing and the measures taken to resolve these issues. The emerging subthemes include religious and cultural beliefs; immigration and lack of social connections; contentment; and faith and spirituality.

Yemi, Layo, and Martha described how religious and cultural beliefs from Nigeria may threaten one's wellbeing, especially if one is not open minded to new beliefs and knowledge of the host country. Some of the issues mentioned were resisting therapy, religious fanaticism, inattention to healthy diet and exercise, and prevalence of gender roles.

Yemi commented:

As Nigerians, I think that our upbringing, our culture and religious beliefs affect our wellbeing whether we like to admit it or not. Our religious beliefs and culture are intertwined and ingrained in us from when we were little and now as adults many of us have conflicting thoughts and views about what we were told while we were growing up, what the church says, what the current society you're living in believes, and what one personally believes. For example, as a Nigerian, when you are at a certain age, the society expects you to marry. If you are not, you begin to feel like a failure. But in Canada, marital status doesn't matter, where you're coming from doesn't matter, and this has changed my view on a lot of things and helped my wellbeing positively. If there's anything I prioritise right now, it is my peace and to be honest with you, if you're able to get that peace sorted out from every other aspect of your life, every other thing would fall in place.

Yemi further described how therapy and other interventions such as exercise and openness to new experiences helped her get better. She reflected:

Nigerians do not embrace therapy or want to discuss mental health issues; they do not take it seriously and they believe such issues are from spiritual attacks. I went through a major life changing experience and although it's not a Nigerian thing to embrace therapy, surprisingly I did. Being able to talk about things and not to bottle things up has been doing a lot of good for me. I think I had to shed a lot of our cultural beliefs, even some religious beliefs. Some of the biases that I had..., some of them are unconscious..., and I had to take ownership...I used to have anxiety and they're always over mundane things but things got better after I prioritised taking care of myself physically, mentally, financially, being very careful about

> *the people I let into my bubble because I realise that other people's actions tend to have a strong effect on me. I started exercising even though exercise is not really a 'Nigerian thing' and being open and accountable to myself have helped me.*

The women described how being an immigrant challenged their wellbeing. Martha described how tensions could arise in the families of new migrants because all members of the household are stressed and trying to settle into their new society. She stated:

> *Africans are social, so moving to a new country and you really don't know so many people, you're faced with a different culture. As an African woman, we tend to look up to our families for support. For example, the man you're married to, for some emotional support, finances, and all of that. But coming to a new culture, we're all struggling right? Even the man is struggling. So, tensions would arise in families of new immigrants.*

Martha further explained how lack of sufficient social connections in the new country challenges the wellbeing of immigrants. She reflected:

> *Immigration is stressful. I have never been as stressed in my entire life as I have been in these three years of living in Canada. Although people back home in Nigeria may complain about the living conditions, but when you're living in a developed country where you don't get as much social support where you can't just leave your kids with the neighbours, the kids can't just go on the streets and play, that is really stressful.*

Echoing the same concern, Layo commented:

> *It is difficult to have a good social life in Canada as an immigrant with kids. I have to take my kids with me everywhere. We don't have enough friends and family to support us like we had in Nigeria.*

Most of the women described themselves as the primary care provider at home. They described how working multiple jobs and taking care of the household threaten their wellbeing. In describing how she manages this, Layo commented:

> *Working full time and being a business owner is stressful. To help me manage the stress, sometimes instead of cooking, I order cooked food in bulk for my family. I also started exercising and I noticed that when I started being serious about my diet and exercising regularly, it positively impacted my mood and my wellbeing.*

Reflecting on stress experienced from the business which negatively impacts her wellbeing, Damola explained her coping strategy thus:

> *The business is stressful based on other commitments that are also competing for my time. I feel like I should put in all my time and effort in the business, but with the nature of my full-time employment – a software product manager... it is impossible. One way I cope with this stress is by not meeting the timeline commitment. I'm not happy about that but, I'm prioritising my health, and time spent with my family and my kids. Whatever time I have left, is what I'm giving the business. I'm giving myself a lot of grace.*

Similarly, Martha described how she maintains her wellbeing by taking time off and asking for help. She commented:

> *I feel taking it one day at a time and being consistent is what has helped me. And whenever I know I've reached my breaking point, I ask for help. I take time off my other job and the business to rest when I need to, so I can enjoy being with the kids or just to enjoy summer. Making those adjustments helped my mental state, and also gave me the rest that I needed.*

The women referred to contentment as an influential factor that helps to maintain their wellbeing. Layo commented:

> *I would say one of the factors that contributes to my positive experience is contentment. This is because being an independent consultant comes with the opportunity to do multiple jobs. That would mean that I have more money which is good, but it also means that I have less time, and I'm more stressed. In the past, I've been stressed, and I've seen the impact on my wellbeing and the family. So, I would rather choose to be content with whatever I am earning on one contract than have multiple contracts, making a lot of money, but every other aspect of my life is suffering.*

Martha pointed out the danger of lack of contentment for immigrant entrepreneurs and recognised it as a potential stressor with huge negative impacts on wellbeing. She reflected:

> *As immigrants, living in Canada gives us access to a lot of opportunities. I don't know if we abuse it by working too hard trying to be successful...putting undue pressure on ourselves to outperform each other. Other Nigerians will advise you to create multiple streams of income, but there are times when that is not feasible because as an individual, there's only so much you can do.*

All the women described themselves as Christians, and three of them reflected on how their faith in God gives them a sense of peace, joy, and contentment.

According to Damola:

> *Life is not perfect, but I would say I'm fulfilled; I wouldn't say I'm happy all the time. There'll be a lot of things..., challenges ... that will threaten your happiness. I'm a Christian. There's a joy I get when I spend time with God and the Holy Spirit. It doesn't necessarily mean that I will always be happy, but even in my unhappiness, I still find joy. I am heavy on gratitude to God. I think my faith has always helped me to thrive irrespective of the country I'm in. As a Christian, no matter what trouble I'm going through or whatever is stealing my happiness, I find joy in the Lord, and I know that all the challenges I face are temporary.*

Similarly, Layo commented:

> *I would say that my sense of contentment comes from my spirituality as a Christian. I know that contentment together with Godliness are great virtues. And even though I aspire for more in life, I don't want to lose myself on my spiritual journey and I know I cannot be stranded because I have a God who takes care of me.*

Martha reflected on the reality of being a Nigerian immigrant woman entrepreneur in Canada and said: "*I wouldn't say I am 100% happy but I find happiness in the little things. As an immigrant female in Canada, I feel like we need more avenues to be seen and heard*".

Discussion

This chapter shows that NWIEs in Canada are mostly pulled into entrepreneurship by positive factors, perceptions of desirability and feasibility which makes them opportunity entrepreneurs, not necessity-based entrepreneurs. This is contrary to findings reported by the Women Entrepreneurship Knowledge Hub (2022) that immigrant women entrepreneurs are often pushed into entrepreneurship due to unfavourable traditional employment requirements in the host country. The motivations driving entrepreneurship are diverse and multifaceted, influenced by personal aspirations, cultural connections, and societal impacts. In the findings presented, women entrepreneurs expressed a variety of motivations for starting their businesses, including the pursuit of self-fulfilment, cultural preservation, and contribution to their communities (Duan et al., 2023). For instance, some participants emphasised the desire to reconnect with their Nigerian roots and promote African culture through their ventures, reflecting intrinsic motivations rooted in personal identity and cultural pride (Duan et al., 2023). Others highlighted the importance of financial stability and the fulfilment derived from pursuing their passions and hobbies (Gielnik et al., 2019). Additionally, societal expectations and the need for validation were cited as motivators, particularly for women entrepreneurs seeking to make meaningful contributions to their households and communities (Johannisson, 2011). These findings resonate with the literature on entrepreneurial passion, which emphasises the role of intrinsic motivation and identity-related emotions in driving venture initiation (Cardon & Kirk, 2015). Entrepreneurial passion not only fosters higher intentions to start a business but also stimulates creativity, persistence, and resourcefulness during the entrepreneurial process (Ferreira-Neto et al., 2023). Moreover, the expression of passion serves as a positive signal to investors, highlighting the entrepreneur's dedication and commitment to their venture (Cardon & Kirk, 2015). Overall, the motivations underlying entrepreneurship are complex and varied, shaped by individual experiences, cultural influences, and societal expectations, underscoring the multifaceted nature of entrepreneurial endeavours.

The concept of wellbeing is inherently subjective, influenced by various factors that shape individuals' perceptions and experiences. In the findings presented, participants described wellbeing as a multifaceted construct encompassing physical health, family dynamics, social connections, and financial stability. These descriptions underscore the subjective nature of wellbeing as individuals interpret and prioritise different aspects of their lives based on personal values and circumstances (Durand, 2015). Moreover, attributes and influences such as family relationships, social connections, and work arrangements were identified as significant contributors to wellbeing. For instance, participants highlighted the importance of flexible work arrangements and entrepreneurship in enhancing their wellbeing by providing autonomy, financial stability, and fulfilment (Rashmi & Kataria, 2022). These findings align with the existing literature, which emphasises the subjective nature of wellbeing and its dependence on various socio-economic, cultural, and personal factors (Diener, 2009). Additionally, studies have shown that demographic factors such as age, gender, and race/ethnicity can influence individuals' perceptions of wellbeing, with mixed findings indicating diverse experiences across different demographic groups (Das et al., 2020). Furthermore, socio-economic status (SES), including income, education, and employment, has been identified as a crucial determinant of wellbeing, with higher SES often associated with greater subjective wellbeing (Das et al., 2020). Religion and culture also play significant roles in shaping individuals' wellbeing through psychological mechanisms, coping strategies, and conceptualisations of happiness (Shiah et al., 2016). Overall, the subjective nature of wellbeing underscores the importance of considering individual perspectives and contextual factors in understanding and promoting holistic wellbeing within diverse populations.

The challenges faced by entrepreneurs, particularly immigrant entrepreneurs (NWIEs), significantly impact their wellbeing and business operations.

While NWIEs may experience higher income and more family time, they also encounter stressors such as gender roles, family care duties, limited social support, and funding constraints. These stressors often compel NWIEs, especially women, to maintain other jobs for financial stability, straining their time and finances and potentially harming their wellbeing (Binder & Coad, 2016; Sevä et al., 2016). Additionally, immigrant entrepreneurs must navigate cultural and religious adjustments, necessitating openness to new experiences and challenging their preconceived beliefs (Mohamed et al., 2004). Despite these challenges, spirituality plays a crucial role in mitigating stress and guiding entrepreneurial decision-making. Studies show that spirituality fosters a sense of purpose and meaning in entrepreneurial endeavours, encouraging entrepreneurs to prioritise societal betterment over mere financial gains (Agarwal & Lenka, 2015). For NWIEs, spirituality serves as a framework for integrating moral, social, and religious values into business practices, contributing to a sense of community and self- actualisation (Farouk, 2011; Villares-Varela & Sheringham, 2020). Entrepreneurs driven by spiritual beliefs demonstrate a commitment to responsible business behaviour, emphasising honesty, integrity, and societal welfare in their decision-making processes (Gill et al., 2018). Consequently, understanding the intersection of spirituality and entrepreneurship among immigrant entrepreneurs is vital for promoting holistic wellbeing and sustainable business practices in diverse communities. By acknowledging the role of spirituality in shaping immigrant entrepreneurs' experiences and decisions, policymakers and stakeholders can better support their integration and success in host countries.

The positive impact of work-life balance on entrepreneurs, particularly women entrepreneurs, is paramount in fostering self-fulfilment and overall wellbeing. Research indicates that entrepreneurship offers a unique avenue for individuals to attain flexibility in managing their time, which can be a significant motivator for venturing into entrepreneurial endeavours. This flexibility enables entrepreneurs to achieve a harmonious balance between their professional pursuits and personal obligations, contributing to their overall satisfaction and eudaimonic wellbeing (Binder & Coad, 2016; Sevä et al., 2016). Women entrepreneurs, in particular, often find themselves juggling multiple roles, including those dictated by gender norms and family care duties, which can lead to heightened stress levels (Diaz-Garcia & Brush, 2012). However, by embracing entrepreneurship, individuals, especially women, can tailor their schedules to accommodate both work and family responsibilities, thereby mitigating the negative effects of work-family conflict (Kim & Ling, 2001; Kirkwood & Tootell, 2008). The ability to work from home and set flexible schedules empowers women entrepreneurs to allocate time judiciously between their business endeavours and domestic duties, enhancing their overall quality of life (Lombard, 2001). Despite the challenges associated with balancing work and family life, entrepreneurship offers a pathway for individuals, particularly women, to navigate these complexities and attain a sense of fulfilment and wellbeing. Therefore, fostering an environment that supports work-life balance initiatives among entrepreneurs, coupled with targeted support for women entrepreneurs, is essential for promoting their overall success and wellbeing in both their professional and personal lives.

Conclusion

The insights garnered from NWIE in Canada have provided a nuanced understanding of wellbeing and its intersection with entrepreneurship. This chapter has illuminated the diverse perspectives of NWIEs, each influenced by cultural, faith, family, and entrepreneurial aspects of their lives. Their contributions to both the practice and the literature are noteworthy and offer valuable implications for policy and research.

The findings presented in this chapter offer substantial contributions to the field. Three insights particularly stand out. First, this chapter uncovers how flexible working conditions and work-life balance of NWIEs aid the creation of business ventures and lead to eudaimonic wellbeing. Second, this chapter uncovers the role of faith and spirituality in the wellbeing of NWIEs, often acting as an ethical or moral compass and capable of creating a sense of contentment in immigrants preventing them from abusing opportunities and privileges in the host country. The third insight highlights the importance of cautious application of religious and cultural principles from an immigrant's home country and the need to be open to new beliefs and practices of the host country.

This chapter enhances the understanding of wellbeing for immigrant women entrepreneurs by emphasising the importance of an intersectional perspective, shedding light on the unique challenges faced by immigrant women in Canada's labour market. By recognising these dynamics, policymakers and support organisations can better tailor interventions to improve the wellbeing of immigrant entrepreneurs, particularly women of colour. For example, one implication of being opportunity entrepreneurs is that the NWIEs do not embrace entrepreneurship as their primary occupation. They engage in the business venture as a "side hustle" making it easy to exit the business and focus on other forms of employment. Although taking time away from the business venture temporarily or permanently may give the entrepreneur time to rest and recuperate, the failure or loss of their business may cause them some distress and could affect their overall wellbeing negatively. Therefore, there is a need to find ways to make entrepreneurship more appealing to these group of women as a sustainable career choice and a reliable source of income. It is also important to explore how to help these women alleviate the entrepreneurial challenges mentioned. Perhaps this will encourage them to favour entrepreneurship over other employment options.

Furthermore, our findings align with the theory of subjective wellbeing, highlighting the inherently personal nature of wellbeing and stressing the need for nuanced, context-specific approaches to support immigrant women entrepreneurs. The experiences of NWIEs offer a valuable entry point for understanding the complexities of the intersection of immigrant entrepreneurship and wellbeing. Future research should explore these dynamics in even greater detail, considering the specific challenges faced by immigrant women entrepreneurs. Moreover, the policy implications drawn from this chapter should be considered seriously, aiming to address disparities and promote inclusive support systems for immigrant entrepreneurs. This inclusive approach will not only benefit the individuals but also contribute to the growth and cohesion of Canada's economy and society.

References

Agarwal, S., & Lenka, U. (2015). Study on work-life balance of women entrepreneurs–review and research agenda. *Industrial and Commercial Training, 47*(7), 356–362.

Amit, K., & Litwin, H. (2010). The subjective well-being of immigrants aged 50 and older in Israel. *Social Indicators Research, 98,* 89–104.

Benz, M., & Frey, B. S. (2008). Being independent is a great thing: Subjective evaluations of self-employment and hierarchy. *Economica, 75*(298), 362–383.

Binder, M., & Coad, A. (2016). How satisfied are the self-employed? A life domain view. *Journal of Happiness Studies, 17*(4), 1409–1433.

Block, J., & Koellinger, P. (2009). I can't get no satisfaction—Necessity entrepreneurship and procedural utility. *Kyklos, 62*(2), 191–209.

Block, S., Galabuzi-Grace, E., & Tranjan, R. (2019). *Canada's colour coded income inequality* (pp. 1–26). Ottawa: Canadian Centre for Policy Alternatives.

Brooks, J., McCluskey, S., Turley, E., & King, N. (2015). The utility of template analysis in qualitative psychology research. *Qualitative Research in Psychology, 12*(2), 202–222.

Cardon, M. S., & Kirk, C. P. (2015). Entrepreneurial passion as mediator of the self–efficacy to persistence relationship. *Entrepreneurship Theory and Practice, 39*(5), 1027–1050.

Cardon, M. S., & Patel, P. C. (2015). Is stress worth it? Stress-related health and wealth trade-offs for entrepreneurs. *Applied Psychology, 64*(2), 379–420.

Das, K. V., Jones-Harrell, C., Fan, Y., Ramaswami, A., Orlove, B., & Botchwey, N. (2020). Understanding subjective well-being: Perspectives from psychology and public health. *Public Health Reviews, 41*(1), 1–32.

Díaz-García, M. C., & Brush, C. (2012). Gender and business ownership: Questioning "what" and "why". *International Journal of Entrepreneurial Behavior & Research, 18*(1), 4–27.

Diener, E. (1984). Subjective well-being. *Psychological Bulletin, 95*(3), 542.

Diener, E. (2009). *The science of well-being: The collected works of Ed Diener* (Vol. 37, pp. 11–58). New York: Springer.

Diener, E., Suh, E. M., Lucas, R. E., & Smith, H. L. (1999). Subjective well-being: Three decades of progress. *Psychological Bulletin, 125*(2), 276.

Duan, C., Kotey, B., & Sandhu, K. (2023). A systematic literature review of determinants of immigrant entrepreneurship motivations. *Journal of Small Business & Entrepreneurship, 35*(4), 599–631.

Durand, M. (2015). The OECD better life initiative: How's life? And the measurement of well-being. *Review of Income and Wealth, 61*(1), 4–17.

Essers, C. (2009). Reflections on the narrative approach: Dilemmas of power, emotions and social location while constructing life-stories. *Organization, 16*(2), 163–181.

Etter-Lewis, G. (1991). Black women's life-stories: Reclaiming self in narrative texts. In S. B. Gluck & D. Patai (Eds.), *Women's words: The feminist practice of oral history* (pp. 43–58). London: Routledge.

Farouk, U. K. (2011). Through the eyes of one woman: Does spirituality have a place in entrepreneurship behavior. *Journal of Global Entrepreneurship, 1*(1), 1–12.

Ferreira-Neto, M. N., de Carvalho Castro, J. L., de Sousa-Filho, J. M., & de Souza Lessa, B. (2023). The role of self-efficacy, entrepreneurial passion, and creativity in developing entrepreneurial intentions. *Frontiers in Psychology, 14,* 1134618.

Gielnik, M. M., Barabas, S., Frese, M., Namatovu-Dawa, R., & Scholz, F. A. (2019). A temporal analysis of entrepreneurial passion and entrepreneurial satisfaction. *Entrepreneurship Theory and Practice*, *43*(2), 296–324.

Gill, A., & Mathur, N. (2018). Religious beliefs and the promotion of socially responsible entrepreneurship in the Indian agribusiness industry. Journal of Agribusiness in Developing and Emerging Economies, *8*(1), 201–218.

Immigration, Refugees and Citizenship Canada (IRCC). (2022). Canada welcomes historic number of newcomers in 2022. Retrieved from https://www.canada.ca/en/immigration-refugees-citizenship/news/2022/12/canada-welcomes-historic-number-of-newcomers-in-2022.html

Johannisson, B. (2011). Towards a practice theory of entrepreneuring. *Small Business Economics*, *36*(2), 135–150.

Kim, J. L. S., & Ling, C. S. (2001). Work-family conflict of women entrepreneurs in Singapore. *Women in Management Review*, *16*(5), 204–221.

Kirkwood, J., & Tootell, B. (2008). Is entrepreneurship the answer to achieving work–family balance? *Journal of Management & Organization*, *14*(3), 285–302.

Lombard, K. V. (2001). Female self-employment and demand for flexible, nonstandard work schedules. *Economic Inquiry*, *39*(2), 214–237.

Mohamed, A. A, Wisnieski, J., Askar, & Syed. (2004). Towards a theory of spirituality in the workplace. *Competitiveness Review: An International Business Journal*, *14*(1/2), 102–107.

Ng, E. S., & Gagnon, S. (2020). *Employment gaps and underemployment for racialized groups and immigrants in Canada: Current findings and future directions*. Toronto: Public Policy Forum.

Nikolaev, B. N., Lerman, M. P., Boudreaux, C. J., & Mueller, B. A. (2023). Self-employment and eudaimonic well-being: The mediating role of problem-and emotion-focused coping. *Entrepreneurship Theory and Practice*, *47*(6), 2121–2154.

OECD. (2017). Policies for stronger and more inclusive growth in Canada. https://www.oecd.org/content/dam/oecd/en/publications/reports/2017/06/policies-for-stronger-and-more-inclusive-growth-in-canada_g1g7b949/9789264277946-en.pdf

Okeke-Ihejirika, P. E., Nkrumah, A., Amoyaw, J., & Otoo, K. (2023). Black entrepreneurship in Western Canada: The push and pull factors. *Journal of Global Entrepreneurship Research*, *13*(1), 17.

Rashmi, K., & Kataria, A. (2022). Work–life balance: A systematic literature review and bibliometric analysis. *International Journal of Sociology and Social Policy*, *42*(11/12), 1028–1065.

Ryan, R. M., & Deci, E. L. (2001). On happiness and human potentials: A review of research on hedonic and eudaimonic well-being. *Annual Review of Psychology, 52*(1), 141–166.

Ryff, C. D. (2017). Eudaimonic well-being, inequality, and health: Recent findings and future directions. *International Review of Economics, 64,* 159–178.

Salami, B., Mason, A., Salma, J., Yohani, S., Amin, M., Okeke-Ihejirika, P., & Ladha, T. (2020). Access to healthcare for immigrant children in Canada. *International Journal of Environmental Research and Public Health, 17*(9), 3320.

Sevä, J. I., Larsson, D., & Strandh, M. (2016). The prevalence, characteristics and well-being of "necessity" self-employed and "latent" entrepreneurs: Findings from Sweden. *International Journal of Entrepreneurship and Small Business, 28*(1), 58–77.

Shir, N. (2015). Entrepreneurial well-being: The payoff structure of business creation. Sweden: Stockholm School of Economics. https://staffstream.hhs.se/public/stream-document.ashx?dl=02240_006

Statistic Canada. (2023). *Immigrant.* Retrieved from: https://www23.statcan.gc.ca/imdb/p3Var.pl?Function=Unit&Id=85107

Stephan, U. (2018). Entrepreneurs' mental health and well-being: A review and research agenda. *Academy of Management Perspectives, 32*(3), 290–322.

Truong, N. K., & Sweetman, A. (2018). Basic information and communication technology skills among Canadian immigrants and non-immigrants. Canadian Public Policy, *44*(S1), S91–S112.

Uy, M. A., Sun, S., & Foo, M. D. (2017). Affect spin, entrepreneurs' well-being, and venture goal progress: The moderating role of goal orientation. *Journal of Business Venturing*, 32(4), 443–460.

Villares-Varela, M., & Sheringham, O. (2020). *Religion, migration and business: Faith, work and entrepreneurialism in the UK.* 1–118, Palgrave: Springer Nature.

Women Entrepreneurship Knowledge Hub. (2022). The state of women's entrepreneurship in Canada 2022. Retrieved from: https://wekh.ca/wp-content/uploads/2022/03/WEKH_State_of_Womens_Entrepreneurship_in_Canada_2022-1.pdf

Index

Note: **Bold** page numbers refer to tables and *italic* page numbers refer to figures.

www.ingramcontent.com/pod-product-compliance
Lightning Source LLC
LaVergne TN
LVHW010939110826
845149LV00013B/2666
9781032535081